Irises

Irises

Sidney Linnegar and
Jennifer Hewitt

CASSELL
ILLUSTRATED

THE ROYAL HORTICULTURAL SOCIETY

The right of Sidney Linnegar & Jennifer Hewitt to be
identified as the authors of this work has been asserted by
them in accordance with the Copyright, Designs and Patents
Act 1988.

First published in Great Britain in 2003 by
Cassell Illustrated
Octopus Publishing Group
2–4 Heron Quays, London E14 4PJ

A CIP catalogue record for this book is available
from the British Library
ISBN 1 84403 018 0

Designer: Justin Hunt
Commissioning Editor: Camilla Stoddart

Printed in China

CONTENTS

Title page:
The vibrant tall
bearded iris
'Champagne Waltz'

INTRODUCTION

There are few families of plants whose members can be found in flower throughout the year in almost any type of soil, situation or climate, and in a wide range of colours and heights from a few centimetres to over 2 m (6 ft). Irises are supreme in all these respects and the majority are easy to grow – although challenges, too, can be found.

The petal edges of tall bearded iris 'Paradise Saved' are laced (very finely serrated).

Irises lighten winter days, herald and celebrate the spring, produce an explosion of colour in the early summer, with the chance of more flowers continuing, together with long-lasting seedheads, and then finally, there is the appearance of the earliest winter-flowering plants.

With over 200 species, native to habitats throughout the temperate regions of the northern hemisphere, from the Arctic Circle to the subtropics, from near-desert conditions to shallow water sites, there are irises for just about anywhere in the garden. And from these species, hybridizers have developed thousands of cultivars. Except for true red (and breeding is bringing that goal ever closer), the whole spectrum of colour can be found; it is not for nothing that the genus takes its name from a Greek goddess whose symbol is the rainbow, and, like all goddesses, the flowers carry an aura of mystery and glamour.

Pacific Coast irises like a cool, lime-free soil and some shade, so make good companions for hostas and other perennials.

HISTORY

It was not only the Greeks who revered the form and colours of the iris; to the Egyptians it was a symbol of power and majesty, and there are representations of irises on pharaohs' sceptres and among the reliefs in the temple of Tutmosis III at Karnak. The oldest pictured iris is in a fresco at Knossos in Crete and the flowers were a favourite decorative motif in both eastern and western art and crafts. The Romans dedicated the iris to Juno, wife of Jupiter, and in medieval times it was particularly associated with the Virgin Mary and the birth of Christ, often appearing in religious paintings. Irises were so widely planted on graves in Muslim countries that today the original habitat and even species status of some is uncertain.

Medicinal uses of the iris were first recorded by the Greeks and it continued to be valued for centuries. The rhizome, or orris root, was also important in perfumery and, although the production of orris in Italy is now declining as synthetic alternatives are taking over, Chianti wine is still given its distinctive flavour by orris root.

Irises were always grown for the beauty of their flowers. Different species were recognized and described in the late 16th century. Linnaeus, who named all the then known species in 1753, listed just 24, but from that time botanists have found and named an increasing number, something that still continues, as does the work of classification. Although all irises share some characteristics, the genus is so diverse that it has been divided into subgenera and sections of closely related species. DNA investigations are now revealing more about these relationships and may well result in the present classification being revised.

Some of the earlier 'species' were, in fact, forms or variants of true species and there were also natural hybrids, occurring where compatible species grew close together in the wild or gardens. In France in the 19th century garden, cultivars began appearing; whether they were the results of man- or bee-made pollinations is not known, but they were popular and other nurserymen in Europe followed the French lead, with notable hybridizers working in Holland and Britain. In America, too, hybridizers began work, in particular on bearded cultivars;

Planted beside, but not in, water at Wakehurst Place, Sussex, are 'double' cultivars of Japanese irises.

Japanese iris cultivars, here planted with ferns beside a pool at Wakehurst Place in Sussex, are viewed effectively from raised walkways.

before long they were the leading producers, as in general they are today, although there are successful breeders in European countries including Britain, and in Australia and New Zealand.

With one exception, the breeding of beardless irises has lagged behind that of the more showy bearded varieties, although most sections now have their devotees producing an ever wider range of cultivars. The exception is Japan, where the native *Iris ensata* (formerly *I. kaempferi*) has been grown and revered in temples and gardens, not least those of the emperors, for 500 years. Wild variants were eagerly sought and brought into cultivation and new cultivars were and still are prized.

ECOLOGY

The majority of irises come from temperate parts of the northern hemisphere, although *I. setosa* occurs almost as far

north as the Arctic Circle, while *I. speculatrix* and *I. formosana* grow close to the subtropics in the Far East. Members of Subgenus *Iris*, the bearded or Pogon irises (see p.16), inhabit open areas of southern Europe from the Atlantic eastwards into central Asia, areas that are fairly dry, certainly in summer. Although some are found at quite high altitudes, they are not

The trial of tall bearded irises at RHS Garden Wisley, large clumps in full bloom in their third year.

true alpines. The Oncocyclus irises (see p.36), from semi-desert parts of the Middle East, are not easy to grow in a maritime climate like that of Britain, although cultivation under glass is possible, as it is for the Regelias (see p.36), which are from mountainous sites in central Asia.

The beardless irises, Subgenus *Limniris* (see p.38), come from very diverse sites and conditions, and so differ greatly in their cultivation requirements. Suitable habitats can include standing or slow-moving water, permanently or seasonally moist soil, as well as Mediterranean climate areas with mainly mild, damp winters and warm to hot, dry summers.

Iris tectorum is one of the hardier crested irises, but needs to be well fed and given some shelter.

Bulbous irises (see p.70) are mostly found in places with winter and spring rainfall or snow but which are baked dry in summer.

There are no true irises native to the southern hemisphere where other members of the family

Dutch iris 'Apollo' has bold flowers. It is a strong grower and its bulbs increase well.

Iridaceae such as *Watsonia*, *Moraea* and *Schizostylis* are found. Other relatives include *Crocus*, *Gladiolus* and *Sisyrinchium*.

THE IRIS PLANT

Irises store food in rhizomes or bulbs, and these grow at or below the soil surface. Rhizomes usually grow horizontally and vary in size from very short and slim to up to 18cm (7in) long and 5cm (2in) thick. Roots grow from the end and underside of the rhizome, starting as fairly thick and fleshy, then developing a network of fine feeding roots not far below the soil surface. Among the Evansia or crested irises (Section Lophiris), there are species that store food in upright stems or 'canes', rather than in rhizomes.

Other subgenera have typical bulbs: these include the Reticulatas (Subgenus *Hermodactyloides*) and the popular Dutch, Spanish and English irises (Subgenus *Xiphium*). Juno irises (Subgenus *Scorpiris*) have very fleshy roots in which they store food as well as in the bulb itself. Most bulbous irises increase by producing bulblets at the base of the parent bulb. Exceptions to this general rule are members of Subgenus *Nepalensis*, which produce a growth bud with fleshy roots attached, and some irises – bearded and beardless – that increase by producing new rhizomes at the ends of underground stolons.

The leaves of rhizomatous irises grow in fans from the active ends of the rhizomes, usually vertically, some arching over at their tips. The larger the rhizome, the taller and stouter the stem

11

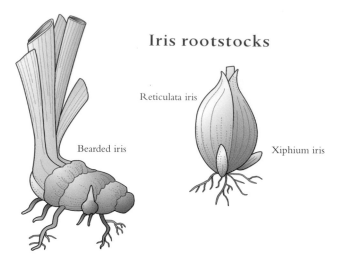

Iris rootstocks

Reticulata iris

Bearded iris

Xiphium iris

and the larger the flowers it can produce as it can store more food. Once a rhizome has bloomed, the main fan of leaves dies, but by then growing points have begun to appear at its sides; these develop into flowering-size rhizomes, although this may take more than one year. The leaves vary in length and in width, from very narrow and grass-like to broad swords, and can be green or tinged with blue or yellow, some with red bases and others variegated lengthways with yellow or white, or a mixture of these. The leaves of bulbous irises grow from the centre of the bulb and may sheathe the stem or be separate from it.

A study of the variation between the parts of the flowers of different irises immediately reveals why there is a division into bearded and beardless. The lines of soft hairs on the upper (inner) parts of the falls are the 'beards' of Pogon, or bearded, irises; the Apogons or beardless irises lack these hairs but usually have a patch of different colour and pattern in this area, known as the signal. Evansia, or crested irises have a ridge or cockscomb in place of the beard; many Junos have a prominent ridge. The beard or lack of it is not the only reason for the division into bearded and beardless: members of each group also have broadly similar cultivation requirements, which differ between the two groups (see the individual chapters on each group for more details).

Everything in iris flowers comes in threes. The three outer petals (or sepals, botanically speaking) are called the falls; they may arch or hang downwards or flare more or less horizontally.

Iris rootstocks

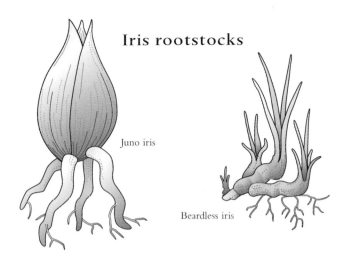

Juno iris

Beardless iris

The three inner, true, petals are the standards. They are usually, but not always, upright; they point downwards in the Junos, and in a few cases are just tiny bristles. The style in the centre of the flower is quite unlike that of most flowers: it branches into three very noticeable petaloid (petal-like) arms, which arch over the inner parts (hafts) of the falls and are often beautifully coloured. On the underside, just below the upward-curling crest, each style arm has a small, even tiny, lip – the end of the stigma. When pollen is put on this lip, it grows down the style to the ovary below the flower, which is divided into three parts containing the ovules. Fertilized by pollen, these ovules develop into seeds. The pollen-bearing anthers are found between the style arms and fall hafts.

Irises for flower arranging

Bulbous Dutch irises provide blue flowers that can be produced all year round as they can be forced or retarded, but growing your own gives different colours in early summer and you can extend the season by adding Spanish irises and *I. latifolia*. *Hermodactylus tuberosus*, an irid with green and black flowers, is easy in sunny, dry places.

For large arrangements with impact, tall bearded irises make a great impression and tall Spurias are effective too, but can drop nectar and need a disposable sheet under the container. Flowers that open later may be smaller and paler but the whole stem normally lasts a reasonable time.

The scent of a few *I. unguicularis* flowers in a warm room is

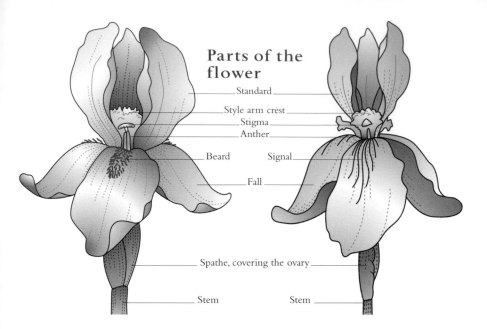

Parts of the flower

Standard
Style arm crest
Stigma
Anther
Beard
Signal
Fall
Spathe, covering the ovary
Stem   Stem

Bearded iris (left);
beardless iris (right)

delightful, and they and other beardless irises, Pacific Coast and Siberians for example, are worth close examination. For Japanese-style arrangements, other irises as well as *I. ensata* are suitable.

Iris foliage, plain or variegated, provides vertical or arching lines and Siberian iris seedheads, as well as those of *I. foetidissima* with its colourful seeds, are useful in dried arrangements.

ABOUT THIS BOOK

Since this is a large and very varied genus, it has been divided into groups that need broadly similar sites and cultivation. Each group has a list of recommended varieties. Most should be obtainable from nurseries. In Britain, an excellent source of information is the *RHS Plant Finder* and there are similar publications in other countries. The internet also contains helpful information.

Where it is available, the recommended varieties are accompanied by information on awards gained after garden trials; many of those recommended have the Royal Horticultural Society's Award of Garden Merit (AGM) and other awards. The RHS AGM is given after trial at RHS Garden Wisley. The British Iris Society (BIS) awards the Dykes Medal (DM) to the best British or European iris, of whatever kind, each year. In the past there was a separate French Dykes

Medal, which might be reinstated at a future date. Currently, Dykes Medals are also the top garden awards made by the American Iris Society (AIS), the Iris Society of Australia and the New Zealand Iris Society.

In the garden	January	February	March	April	May	June	July	August	September	October	November	December
I. unguicularis and cultivars	●	●	●							●	●	●
I. histrioides, I. danfordiae	●	●										
I. reticulata and cultivars		●	●									
Juno irises (hardy)			●	●								
Dwarf bearded species and cultivars				●	●							
Intermediate bearded cultivars					●							
Bearded species (except dwarf)					●	●						
Tall bearded cultivars					●	●						
Bulbous Spanish and Dutch irises				●	●	●						
Pacific Coast species and cultivars					●	●						
Evansia irises (hardy)					●	●						
I. setosa and forms					●							
Siberian irises					●							
Chrysographes species and cultivars						●	●					
I. laevigata and cultivars						●	●					
I pseudacorus, I. versicolor						●	●					
I. foetidissima and forms						●	●					
I. foetidissima seedpods	●	●								●	●	●
Spuria irises						●	●					
Louisiana irises						●	●					
Other beardless irises						●	●					
Japanese irises						●	●	●				
Bulbous English irises						●	●					
Remontant Siberian cultivars					●	●	●	●	●			
Remontant bearded cultivars					●	●		●	●	●		

Under glass	January	February	March	April	May	June	July	August	September	October	November	December
Evansia and Juno irises	●	●	●	●	●							
Aril irises			●	●	●							
Bulbous irises	●	●		●								

Variegated foliage	January	February	March	April	May	June	July	August	September	October	November	December
I. pallida, I. ensata			●	●	●	●	●	●	●			
I. foetidissima, I. japonica	●	●	●	●	●	●	●	●	●	●	●	●
I. pseudacorus				●	●	●						

The iris calendar

BEARDED IRISES

The most important group of bearded irises belongs to subgenus *Iris*. They are often called the Pogon irises or, incorrectly, *Iris germanica*. The AIS is the International Cultivar Registration Authority for rhizomatous irises; it classifies bearded iris cultivars according to height and flowering season. These classifications are:

Miniature Dwarf Bearded (MDB)	*Intermediate Bearded (IB)*
	Miniature Tall Bearded (MTB)
Median Bearded Irises –	*Border Bearded (BB)*
Standard Dwarf Bearded (SDB)	Tall Bearded (TB)

There are two other major groups of bearded irises, the Species and the Arils. The Arils include Oncocyclus, Regelia, Regelio-cyclus (hybrids between the two) and Arilbred (hybrids between Pogons and Arils).

CULTIVATION

All the Pogon irises need a sunny, well-drained position. Although they prefer neutral, or better still, mildly alkaline soil, they can be grown in acid soil, but lime should be added for better results. They will survive in shady places but flower poorly, if at all, without a summer baking, which helps to develop flower buds within the rhizomes. For this reason, they should be planted with the upper part of the rhizomes above soil level (see p.18) on all but very sandy soils, with grit being dug in beforehand if the drainage needs to be improved. They

The vibrant tall bearded iris 'Champagne Waltz', flowering in the International Iris Competition in Florence, has orange beards for extra zest.

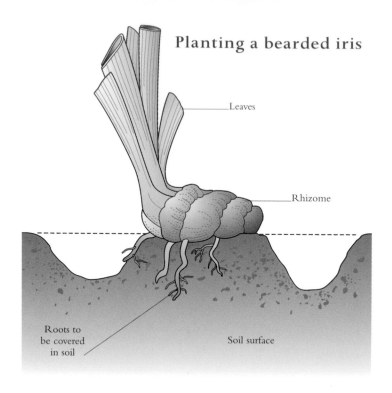

Planting a bearded iris

Leaves

Rhizome

Roots to be covered in soil

Soil surface

grow poorly, and may rot, in ground that stays wet for long periods, while alternating heat and wet in summer encourages fungal diseases. If conditions are very unhelpful (such as heavy clay in areas of high rainfall), raised beds may be successful. In hot climates, deeper planting is necessary to protect the rhizomes in summer. Plant spacings are given under each section; obviously, the taller the plant, the larger it is and the more space it will require.

Mulching is anathema to bearded irises; it encourages rot in the rhizomes and deprives them of sunlight and the essential baking. Well-rotted garden compost, manure, spent hops or mushroom compost are all beneficial if they are dug in before planting, but ensure that a layer of soil tops the mounds on which the rhizomes sit – the lower, feeding roots will find the food. Bonemeal, hoof and horn or a slow-release general fertilizer may be mixed into the top few centimetres (inches) of soil and established plants can be top-dressed in spring with a proprietary fertilizer that is not too high in nitrogen, otherwise there will be leaf growth at the expense of flowers and the

The dwarf bearded species, Iris lutescens *(syn.* I. chamaeiris) *giving a superb display in a raised bed.*

plants can become susceptible to disease. A recommended dressing is one made up of 4 parts by weight of bonemeal, 2 parts superphosphate of lime, 1 part each sulphate of ammonia and sulphate of potash, well mixed and applied at the rate of 60–75g per sq m (2–2½oz per sq yard).

Trim the leaves of new plants or those of newly separated rhizomes when replanting is necessary, to prevent wind-rock until the roots have a good grip on the soil; if rhizomes have no long roots, hold them steady until the roots grow with a short piece of cane, put in behind them, attached with a tie of soft material. On established plants, leaves can be trimmed in late summer or early autumn, but while they are green and helping to feed the rhizomes, it is better, if less tidy, to leave them alone. When they die back naturally, remove them by pulling them away gently and completely.

When flowering finishes, if no seedpods are wanted, cut the stems right back to their bases as stubs can introduce bacterial soft rot (see p.87) into the rhizomes.

Pogon irises look good in beds on their own but both their foliage and flowers make a valuable contribution to mixed plantings. Do not let other plants grow over the rhizomes as this may keep them moist and provide a happy home for slugs and snails. Plants such as heucheras or the less-spreading hardy geraniums can go between clumps of the taller irises and spring bulbs, day lilies and bulbous Dutch or Spanish irises will give a succession of colour. Other good companions are the hardy irids, such as crocosmias and gladioli, and the less-hardy types, which can be added in spring, such as large-flowered gladioli and watsonias. Clumps of pinks (*Dianthus* species and cultivars) make attractive edgings.

Aril irises are so-called as their seeds have a white or cream appendage, the aril, at one end. Some of the species and hybrids belonging to this group are cold-hardy, others are not, and all are very susceptible to too much wet at the wrong times, so they are generally safest grown under glass. Even then they may not be easy in the British climate and similar conditions. Regelio-cyclus irises and Arilbreds may be grown outside in warm areas as long as they are in alkaline soil with first-class drainage and in a sunny, sheltered spot.

Colours and flower forms

The range of colours in bearded cultivars, whatever their size, is very wide and getting wider all the time: white, cream, all shades of yellow, peach, apricot, orange, brown, reds (yellow- or blue-toned), many shades of blue, lavender, lilac, purple, through to black. Two or more colours may occur in a flower, in various combinations and patterns, and beards can add yet another variation. Terms are used to classify these patterns, as follows:

amoena	white standards, coloured falls
bicolor	two colours, other than amoena, neglecta or variegata
bitone	two tones of the same colour
blend	a mixture of colours

luminata	development of the plicata pattern where the darker colour is more solid, often with pale petal edges or a halo around the beard
neglecta	pale blue standards, deeper falls
plicata	white to yellow ground colour, stitched, dotted or veined in a different, darker colour at the petal edges
self	single colour throughout
variegata	yellow standards with red, maroon or brown falls

Broken colours, with darker and lighter, or white streaks in the flowers, are a recent development from the USA, where some people are also working on new cultivars with variegated foliage. The colours above refer to the flowers: irises with striped leaves have the cultivar name 'Variegata' and are not the same thing as the variegata colour pattern, which is derived from the species *I. variegata*.

Ruffled petal edges give an air of gaiety − if not so overdone that flowers can find it difficult to open − and edges can also be laced, with fine serrations. There are now 'space age' irises where extensions on the beards range from horns (points) at the outer ends, to

A wealth of flower on 'Stinger', a 'space age' standard dwarf bearded iris with violet horns.

larger and longer petaloid additions, named spoons and flounces. They are not to everyone's taste, especially the more extreme forms, and it is as well to see them in flower, or a clear photograph of an example, before buying. These plants have not been genetically modified in a laboratory; hybridizers are bringing out genetic potential through planned cross-pollinations.

MINIATURE DWARF BEARDED IRISES (MDB)

These delightful little plants, at under 20cm (8in), are the earliest to flower, starting in April in Britain. Most have two flowers per stem, with open standards showing the heart of the flower. They soon make free-flowering clumps to give a mass of colour. Sunny, well-drained spots on the edges of beds, especially raised beds, in sinks or troughs or the rock garden, are ideal for them. Watch out for slugs and snails.

Being small plants with a limited root system, these irises tend to exhaust the soil around them quite quickly and they should be replanted in improved soil (see p.18) every two years, or three at most, a few weeks after flowering finishes or later in summer. Top-dress in spring at the rate of 60g per sq m (2oz per sq yd).

There is no trial for this group at Wisley and no AGMs have been awarded. The British-raised 'Marhaba' was given a First Class Certificate in 1971; it is a very good deep violet-blue with two or three flowers per stem. Other recommended British MDBs are the plicatas 'Scribe' and 'Dunlin', both with purple markings on a white ground.

Miniature dwarf bearded irises, such as 'Scribe', need a sunny place in a rock garden.

Recommended varieties

'**Alpine Lake**' White standards; very pale blue falls. Height 18cm (7in). Caparne-Welch Medal (AIS).

'**Bee Wings**' Yellow with maroon markings on the falls. Height 15cm (6in).

'**Bright White**' Pure white. Height 18cm (7in).

'**Fashion Lady**' Mid-yellow self. Height 15cm (6in).

'**Garnet Elf**' Dark red self. Height 18cm (7in) Caparne-Welch Medal.

'**Jasper Gem**' Brownish-red bitone. Height 20cm (8in).

'**Knick Knack**' White and pale purple plicata. Height 15cm (6in).

'**Lemon Puff**' Lemon standards; white falls. Height 15cm (6in). Caparne-Welch Medal.

STANDARD DWARF BEARDED IRISES (SDB)

These flower a little later than the miniature dwarfs, producing taller, branched stems from 20–38cm (8–15in), each carrying three to four flowers. With flowers opening in succession, the bloom period of each stem, and the clump, is longer than that of the MDBs (which is, of course, even more true of the taller beardeds). They quickly make good clumps, covered in bloom. The sunny front or edge of a bed is where they will be seen and grow best and they are also happy in a rock garden. Plant and fertilize as for the MDBs. July is a good month for this and for lifting and dividing, which should be done every three years; divide into small clumps of two or three rather than single rhizomes. Set plants 20–25cm (8–10in) apart.

An early cultivar, 'Green Spot' (AGM), appeared in 1951 and is still going strong. It is creamy white with olive-green around the beard. Another older but good one is the bright brown 'Gingerbread Man', which has a violet beard.

Recommended varieties

'**Ballet Lesson**' AGM Peach-pink, falls with white centre and beard. Height 30cm (12in).

'**Bedford Lilac**' AGM Lilac-blue standards; falls with a deeper spot. Height 28cm (11in). Cook-Douglas Medal (AIS).

'Bibury' AGM White self. Height 30cm (12in). The only SDB to win the BIS Dykes Medal.

'Bromyard' AGM Blue-grey standards; maroon and yellow falls. Height 30cm (12in).

'Eyebright' AGM Bright yellow with brown lines on the falls. Height 30cm (12in).

'Jeremy Brian' AGM Silver-blue self. Height 25cm (10in).

'Bibury', a standard dwarf bearded iris, has more subtle colouring than a written description can convey.

'Mary McIlroy' AGM Orange-yellow self. Height 30cm (12in).

'Michael Paul' AGM Dark purple self. Height 30cm (12in). Cook-Douglas Medal.

'Morning's Blush' AGM Yellow standards and orange falls and beard. Height 35cm (14in).

'Pale Shades' AGM Blue-tinted standards; buttery-cream falls. Height 30cm (12in).

'Rain Dance' AGM Blue self. Height 25cm (10in). Cook-Douglas Medal.

'Sarah Taylor' AGM Cream standards; primrose falls; blue beard. Height 30cm (12in).

'Sun Doll' AGM Medium yellow self. Height 35cm (14in). Cook-Douglas Medal.

'Sweet Kate' AGM Lemon bitone; falls darker than standards. Height 35cm (14in).

INTERMEDIATE BEARDED IRISES (IB)

The intermediate beardeds overlap with the SDBs and carry on into the tall bearded season. They should have two or more branches and carry at least six flowers on each stem. Their height is from 38–70cm (15–28in) and they need spacing at least 25–35cm (10–14in) apart, and are best suited to beds and borders. Planting and dividing can be done during the three months after flowering has ended.

Two American-bred IBs that have received the AGM are 'Cee Jay', a white plicata with violet rims, and 'Raspberry Blush', rich pink including the beard. Both have also won the Sass Medal from the AIS.

Recommended varieties

'Alison Taylor' AGM Brown plicata on a yellow ground. Height 45cm (18in).

'Bold Stroke' AGM French blue self, blackish beard. Height 60cm (24in).

'Bronzaire' AGM Golden bronze self. Height 50cm (20in).

'Cannington Skies' Ruffled sky-blue self, white beard. Height 45cm (18in).

'Clara Garland' AGM Bright yellow with brown lines on the falls. Height 50cm (20in).

'Fierce Fire' AGM Yellow standards; falls blended red, orange and yellow. Height 58cm (23in).

'Katie-Koo' AGM Deep purple bicolor. Height 50cm (20in).

'Langport Wren' AGM Deep maroon self, brown beard. Height 56cm (22in).

'Magic Bubbles' AGM Coral-pink self. Height 60cm (24in).

'Mary Constance' AGM Excellent deep violet-blue. Height 63cm (25in).

'Maui Moonlight' AGM Bright lemon-yellow self. Height 58cm (23in).

'Prince of Burgundy' AGM Burgundy standards; falls white with burgundy plicating. Height 56cm (22in). May rebloom. Sass Medal.

'Strawberry Love' AGM Rose-pink bitone from Australia. Height 50cm (20in).

'Templecloud' AGM Palest blue standards; violet falls. Height 60cm (24in).

'Whiteladies' AGM Small-flowered white self. Height 43cm (17in).

Elegantly ruffled 'Mary Constance' is one of the best intermediate bearded irises.

Intermediate bearded iris 'Templecloud' is an example of the amoena pattern of colouring, set off here by a bushy brown beard.

MINIATURE TALL BEARDED IRISES (MTB) AND BORDER BEARDED IRISES (BB)

These two groups flower at the same time as the tall beardeds (see p.29) but have shorter stems and smaller flowers. They are useful for providing variety and also in smaller gardens or in windy sites. Miniature Tall Beardeds (known as Table Irises in the USA because of their suitability for flower arranging) have graceful, slender but strong stems with the same height limits as IBs, their branches bearing eight or more flowers. Hybridizing in this group concentrates on maintaining the elegance of the plants, and the flowers may be less ruffled than those of other bearded cultivars, but still have a lively air. As fairly recent arrivals in the trials at Wisley, few have received the AGM but this number is sure to increase as they are good plants.

Cultivate as for other beardeds, setting plants about 30cm (12in) apart. They may take a little longer to settle and, like all Pogons, should be well watered in and kept just moist, especially in dry spells, until growing away.

The Border Beardeds are more robust plants, the same height as the MTBs but with larger flowers and thicker stems, with seven or more flowers. Plant and treat them as for the tall beardeds. Two outstanding plants are the British dark violet on white plicata 'Orinoco Flow' 63cm (25in) and the American 'Brown Lasso', 56cm (22in), with butterscotch standards and violet falls edged with brown. Both have AGMs and have also won the Dykes Medal in their respective countries.

British Dykes medal winner 'Orinoco Flow' is a stunning plicata border bearded iris.

Recommended MTB varieties

'Bumblebee Deelite' AGM Yellow standards; falls deep maroon, edged yellow. Height 45cm (18in). Williamson–White Medal (AIS).

'Carolyn Rose' AGM Fine rose-pink plicata on a white ground. Height 58cm (23in).

'**Chickee**' AGM Pure medium yellow self. Height 48cm (19in).

'**Lady Belle**' AGM White standards, shaded purple at the base; falls white, stitched purple. Height 56cm (22in).

'**Loose Valley**' Recommended for the AGM – to be confirmed when it is in commerce. Maize-yellow standards; cream falls, edged maize with faint, purple plicata markings. Height 56cm (22in).

'**New Idea**' Rosy mulberry self; yellow beard. Height 65cm (26in). Williamson–White Medal.

'**Robin Goodfellow**' AGM Very good pure white self. Height 48cm (19in).

A good clump of miniature tall bearded iris 'Bumblebee Deelite' shows small but striking flowers on slender stems.

'**Welch's Reward**' AGM Yellow standards; red–purple falls, edged yellow. Height 56cm (22in).

Recommended BB varieties

'**Apricot Frosty**' White standards; apricot falls. Height 58cm (23in). Knowlton Medal (AIS).

'**Batik**' White ground, streaked royal-purple. Height 65cm (26in).

'**Blackbeard**' AGM Pale steely blue; purple-black beard. Height 63cm (25in).

'**Cool Treat**' AGM White standards; blue-violet falls. Height 65cm (26in).

'**Cranapple**' AGM Cranberry standards; deeper falls. Height 60cm (24in). Knowlton Medal.

'**Jungle Shadows**' Brown/grey and purple/black blend. Height 65cm (26in). Knowlton Medal.

'**Pink Bubbles**' Light pink self. Height 56cm (22in). Knowlton Medal.

'**Raspberry Sundae**' Mulberry-rose self. Height 65cm (26in). Knowlton Medal.
'**Whoop 'em Up**' Gold standards; maroon falls edged gold. Height 68cm (27in). Knowlton Medal.
'**Zinc Pink**' French-rose self. Height 60cm (24in). Knowlton Medal.

TALL BEARDED IRISES (TB)

Usually, these come most readily to mind when irises are mentioned, with good reason: they are the largest-flowered, most glamorous and most colourful. The three-dimensional, architectural flower has no equal for form, and its exits and entrances have an almost mysterious air. In addition, it is easier to appreciate a flower that comes up to a height at which it can comfortably be seen. Although any bearded iris over 70cm (28in) is classified as a TB, the majority are around 90cm (36in) and many are taller.

Strong stems carry three or four branches and the terminal produces 10–12 flowers in all, which open more or less in succession giving, up to three weeks of bloom per spike, weather permitting. So a clump of several spikes will therefore flower for a month or more. Flowering usually begins in late spring – mid-May in Britain – and lasts for some six weeks.

There are old cultivars, some dating from the 19th century, still giving good service in gardens. These may not have the arching or flaring, and usually ruffled, falls of modern irises, and they lack substance (thickness in the petals) so are easily damaged, but they are long-term survivors that grow and bloom even with minimal care. They will also respond generously to kinder treatment. As well as being more numerous than those of older cultivars, the flowers of modern varieties have better substance so are relatively unaffected by rain and sun. Hailstorms are a different matter, but undamaged buds will open later.

As with the other bearded irises they prefer sunny positions in alkaline soil with a pH of around 7 (see p.16). If more humus is needed, dig it in before planting and remember not to let it touch the rhizomes. Space the plants at least 30–38cm (12–15in) apart. The best time for planting or replanting is fairly soon after they have flowered, although container-grown plants should be put out as soon as possible, at any time between spring and early autumn, as they quickly outgrow their pots. Newly planted TBs with their large leaf fans may need temporary staking (see p.19). If a single rhizome, with only small offsets, flowers in the first year after planting, the spike in full bloom can be more than the roots can hold, especially in windy places. It is worth the time and effort involved in staking them for the current display and so that the plant as a whole can establish itself better.

Repeat-flowering tall bearded irises

Some TB irises are remontant, or repeat-blooming. These need a second feed after their first flowering, which is usually early, and they should be watered in dry spells in summer to encourage the rhizomes to grow to flowering size in late summer and early autumn. They cannot be depended on to rebloom every year in cooler climes, such as Britain, or in countries with very hot summers, but when they do perform, the extra effort in cultivation proves well worthwhile. (At present, not many repeat-flowering median beardeds are available, although they can be found in the USA and are being bred elsewhere.)

Some poplar remontant TBs include:

'Champagne Elegance' White and buff. Height 83cm (33in).
'Dark Rosaleen' AGM Red-black; has frequently rebloomed in the trial beds at Wisley. Height 78cm (31in).
'Earl of Essex' White and light violet plicata. Height 88cm (35in).
'Provencal' Yellow with red plicating. Height 85cm (34in).
'Repartee' White standards; red falls. Height 75cm (30in).
'Roseplic' Pink standards; white falls, edged pink. Height 85cm (34in).
'Spellbreaker' Violet self. Height 90cm (36in).

Space age irises

The first bearded iris with a horn, 'Unicorn', appeared in America in the 1950s and this trait was developed to produce irises with other extensions on the beards, later christened 'space age'. They became more popular and available in the

The flowers of intermediate bearded iris 'Halloween Rainbow' are in proportion to the height of its stems, and may appear twice a year.

1990s and may sometimes be seen in the Wisley TB Trial. 'Thornbird' (AGM) is a pale ecru and greenish-tan bicolor with a small spoon, 'Conjuration' is white with blue edges, red beards and white horns and 'Mesmerizer' is white with tangerine beards that have white flounces ending in pale green pompons. All three have won the American Dykes Medal. Others in this range include 'Godsend', which has pink standards, pink-and-white falls and amethyst horns; 'Sky Hooks', which is soft yellow with golden beards ending in violet horns and has proved a good grower; and British-bred 'Alien Mist' in palest blue with a blue-violet beard and horns. Among the other iris classifications, 'Stinger' (AGM), a standard dwarf bearded (though it may grow a bit taller) has yellow standards, yellow and white falls with violet stitching and orange beards with deep purple horns. These more elaborate additions are a matter of personal taste.

Recommended TB varieties

'Alizes' AGM White standards; mid-blue falls, French-bred. Height 83cm (33in).

'Annabel Jane' Lilac bitone, Height 120cm (48in). British Dykes Medal.

'Blue Luster' AGM Mid-blue bitone from the USA. Height 98cm (38in).

'Bob Nichol' AGM Buttercup yellow self. Height 90cm (36in).

'Breakers' AGM Well ruffled, true blue self. May rebloom. Height 94cm (37in).

'Cardew' AGM Pale blue standards; red-violet falls. Height 100cm (39in).

'Designer's Choice' AGM White self. Height 80cm (32in).

'Dovedale' AGM Pinkish lilac self. Height 80cm (32in). British DM.

'Alizes', bred in France, is a tall bearded iris whose colour pattern is almost in the luminata category.

'**Dutch Chocolate**' Reddish chocolate self. May rebloom. Height 88cm (35in).

'**Dwight Enys**' AGM Yellow standards; red-brown falls. Height 85cm (34in).

'**Early Light**' AGM Creamy yellow bitone; deeper falls. Height 98cm (38in). British DM.

'**Edith Wolford**' Yellow standards; violet-blue falls. Height 100cm (39in). USA DM.

'**Feu du Ciel**' Bright orange self. Height 88cm (35in).

'**Garlanda**' AGM Biscuit, fading to pale lemon at fall edges. Height 100cm (39in).

'**Jane Phillips**' AGM Historic light blue self; still popular. Height 90cm (36in).

'**Lark Rise**' AGM Grey-blue standards; deep lavender falls. Height 98cm (38in).

'**Meg's Mantle**' AGM Fawn standards; cream falls with magenta plicata markings. Height 83cm (33in).

'**Night Owl**' Purple-black self with velvety falls. Height 98cm (38in).

'**Orange Dawn**' AGM Bright orange bitone. Height 98cm (38in).

'**Princess Sabra**' AGM Shot pink standards; burgundy wine falls. Height 98cm (38in).

'**River Avon**' AGM Ruffled light blue self. Height 100cm (39in).

'**Severn Side**' AGM Chartreuse standards; slate blue falls. Height 90cm (36in).

'**Snowy Owl**' AGM Pure white self including the beards. Height 98cm (38in).

'**Stepping Out**' AGM Older deep purple-blue plicata on white; still popular. Height 98cm (38in). USA DM.

'**Superstition**' AGM Dark reddish-black self. Height 90cm (36in).

'**Tintinara**' AGM Red-brown with a blue flash on the falls. Height 80cm (32in).

'**Titan's Glory**' AGM Bishop's purple self. Height 94cm (37in). USA DM.

'**Vanity**' AGM Pink self. Height 90cm (36in). USA DM.

'**Violet Icing**' AGM Striking violet plicata on white ground. Height 90cm (36in).

'Warleggan' AGM Neglecta, pale blue standards; violet–blue falls. Height 94cm (37in).

'Wensleydale' AGM White standards tinted violet; violet falls. 100cm (39in). British DM.

'Wharfedale' AGM Mid-blue flowers. Height 100cm (39in). British DM.

BEARDED IRIS SPECIES

Tall bearded cultivars are sometimes wrongly called *Iris germanica*. The blue-purple, 75cm (30in) tall iris that has this species name is cultivated in many countries and is now suspected to be of hybrid origin, with a number of forms. Known as the 'old blue flag', it is pretty well indestructible and still popular, may rebloom and has an AGM. The form 'Florentina' (AGM), with whitish flowers, 40cm (16in) tall, was

Iris pallida
'Variegata', with
yellow-striped foliage
and good flowers,
revels in ideal
conditions in
Florence.

one source of orris root. However, the principal source was the light violet-blue, scented *I. pallida*, which was more widely grown around Florence in Italy where the rhizomes were harvested for perfumery and other uses. *I. pallida* is an excellent garden iris reaching 60–90cm (24–36in) in flower and with blue-green leaves that look good for much of the year. It has two foliage variants: 'Variegata' (AGM) with leaves striped lengthwise with yellow, and good flowers, and the white-striped 'Argentea Variegata', attractive but less vigorous and usually with rather poor flowers.

Other tall bearded species are the white-flowered *I. albicans* (AGM), 40cm (16in) tall, much planted on graves in Muslim countries, and *I. variegata* (AGM), yellow standards and red to brown falls. Its form *reginae* is white, veined violet. Both are 40–50cm (16–20in) tall. While these species can be recommended for the majority of gardens – sited and cultivated as for cultivars of similar sizes – other species are more tender or demanding.

Dwarf bearded species played a large part in the development of median and dwarf cultivars but are charming plants in their own right. They need the same conditions as dwarf cultivars and like them may soon exhaust the soil and need replanting.

Purple *I. aphylla* is quite variable in height, from 15–45cm (6–18in) with taller forms having branches. *I. lutescens* (syn. *I. chamaeiris*) (AGM) comes in yellow, white or purple and reaches 8–25cm (3–10in) tall. *I. reichenbachii,* 18cm (7in) tall, is yellow or brownish-purple, and *I. schachtii* has similar height and colouring, as well as a good purple form. Shorter still is *I. pumila* (a name often used for all dwarf beardeds), only 8–13cm (3–5in) high, which as well as violet-purple can be white, yellow, blue or black. *I. suaveolens* (syn. *I. mellita*) is violet, crimson or yellowish and *I. attica* is purple. Both are of a similar height to *I. pumila*. These tiny species are safer in a bulb frame or cold greenhouse as they can be badly damaged by snails and slugs in the open garden.

ARIL IRISES

These bearded species, with arils on the seeds, are found from eastern Europe eastwards to China and Korea and from Siberia in the north to the Himalayas. They are divided into five sections of which Oncocyclus and Regelia are the most important horticulturally, though some Pseudoregelia species are commercially available.

The pure Arils are demanding in cultivation, even under glass. They need a small amount of water in autumn to start root growth but would then, in nature, be covered with snow and stay more or less dry until the spring melt brings ample moisture. At this point, leaves and flowers are quickly produced before hot, dry summers send the plants into dormancy. These conditions can be simulated under glass (see p.78, but for more detailed advice on cultivation, *A Guide to Species: Irises*, is recommended, p.88).

Some Aril irises can be tried outside in warm, dry parts of Britain if excellent drainage (and perhaps overhead cover after flowering) are provided, and in suitable climates elsewhere, the scope is wider. The Regelias, which are slightly less demanding than the Oncocyclus irises, include *I. stolonifera* with cultivars 'Vera', reddish-brown with a blue beard, and 'Zwanenburg Beauty', pale mauve with reddish streaks and one of the easiest to grow. *I. hoogiana* (AGM), another Regelia, is up to 65cm (26in) tall and also stoloniferous. It has pale lavender flowers; white in 'Alba'. The hybrid 'Bronze Beauty' is a brown bitone. Hybrids between the two sections, known as Regelio-cyclus, include: 'Chione', white with blue to grey veining and a dark brown patch on the falls; 'Clotho', deep violet and black including the beard; 'Dardanus' with lilac standards and cream falls veined purple; and 'Theseus', deep violet. All are from 30–40cm (12–16in) tall.

These old cultivars were introduced

Arilbred 'Wine and Lilac' shows Oncocyclus influence in its shape and dark signal but is easier to grow than a pure Aril.

from Holland, mostly in the early 20th century. Now hybridizers concentrate on producing Arilbred irises, hybrids between Arils and Pogons. Those with half or less Aril in their parentage can be tried outside, although even so it is safer in Britain to grow them under cover with good ventilation except in the dryest areas. The old 'Lady Mohr', pale lavender and yellow with crimson markings and brown beard, 75cm (30in) tall, is a good garden iris in dry places.

Newer American Arilbreds include: 'Bionic Comet', 60cm (24in), old gold with a maroon signal and beard (a dark signal on the fall, around the beard, is a feature of Aril species quite often passed on to Arilbreds); 'Desert Dream', 65cm (26in), violet to violet-grey with a black beard; and 'Prophetic Message', 50cm (20in), violet standards and falls blended violet and brown, with bronze beards.

British-raised Arilbreds were listed in the *RHS Plant Finder* quite recently and may appear again; among them were 'Main Sequence', 70cm (28in) tall, yellow bitone with maroon signals and yellow beards; 'Windrider', 78cm (31in) tall, with pale blue standards and pale violet falls with maroon signals and orange beards; and 'Wine and Lilac', 75cm (30in) tall, with lilac standards and lilac-rose falls, burgundy signals and purple beards.

'Chione' is a delightful Regelio-cyclus hybrid for a pot or a warm, well-drained spot in the garden.

BEARDLESS IRISES

The beardless, or Apogon irises belong to Subgenus *Limniris*, which includes the Section Lophiris (crested) irises, as well as the well-known Siberian, Japanese, Pacific Coast and Spuria irises, and those that grow in water or moist soil. Among the species are *Iris unguicularis* and its relatives, which are valued for their winter blooms, and *I. foetidissima*, grown for its colourful, long-lasting seedheads and foliage. A feature of many Apogons is the signal, an area of the falls that is often a different colour from the rest of the sepal. The signal guides insects to the nectar at the base of the falls and style arms, and it is often very decorative.

Among the beardless irises, it is possible to find plants suited to almost any place in any garden. There is a range of cultivars, in addition to the species and hybrids. No general cultivation advice applies to them all – except that, although most will grow in shade, they flower better if they have sun for at least part of the day, especially in summer. Many are the easiest of perennials to grow, combining well with other plants, but some do have special, although not difficult, requirements, and a few of the species present a challenge.

CRESTED IRISES

The crested irises are also known as the Evansias or Section Lophiris. It is not unusual for their flowers to be mistaken for orchids. The ridged crests on the falls can look quite like beards, but they feel less soft. Their rhizomes may grow horizontally on the soil surface, some spreading by stolons, while others produce

Iris japonica in a warm corner of the garden has plenty of flowers above the fans of leaves.

thick vertical stems, or canes, in place of rhizomes. They range from tiny plants to giants 2m (6ft) tall; some are fully hardy, others less so and a few need to be grown under glass (see p.78).

The tiniest species are *I. lacustris* (AGM), only 2–5cm (¾–2in) tall, and *I. cristata* (AGM), taller at 10cm (4in). Native to North America, in open sites or the edges of woods, both are stoloniferous and produce violet-blue flowers that are delicately marked on the falls and have orange or yellow crests in late spring. They prefer a neutral or lime-free soil with ample humus or peat in shade or semi-shade. Well suited to a rock garden or trough or to being grown in pots, they need division and replanting in early autumn every two or three years. Plant in groups of three or four rhizomes linked by their stolons. *I. lacustris* is less easy to keep than *I. cristata*, which has a pretty white form, 'Alba'; other colour variants are appearing in America. There is a good lavender-flowered hybrid between these species.

From Asia comes *I. gracilipes* with slender, branched stems 10–15cm (4–6in) long, bearing several very dainty, starry, lilac-mauve flowers, white in 'Alba'. It needs similar conditions to the two American species, and has been hybridized with *I. lacustris.*

Two other species with horizontal rhizomes are *I. milesii* (AGM) and *I. tectorum*. They make more substantial plants and will grow in most well-drained soils in sunny positions. Both are heavy feeders and, as well as having rich compost dug in before planting, should be top-dressed, with 2cm (¾in) of the same, twice each year, in spring and after flowering. They are hardy in many British gardens but will not tolerate wetter soils. *I. milesii* is a robust plant with stems up to 90cm (36in) tall and much branched, bearing many lilac-pink flowers with darker markings and a gold crest in early summer. It does not need division and replanting as often as *I. tectorum*, which has short roots and grows quickly so needs replanting every other year soon after it flowers in early summer. *I. tectorum* is seen growing on thatched roofs in Japan, although it was probably originally from China. It appreciates some shelter, or is good in a pot if well fed. The flowers are large, medium violet-blue with white crests – there is also a lovely white form – on stems around 30cm (12in) tall. A rare form has variegated leaves, but most offered are, in fact, *I. japonica* 'Variegata' (AGM). 'Burma Form' is darker blue, and 'Paltec', a hybrid with the bearded *I. pallida*, has silvery blue flowers.

The stems of the 'cane' Evansias are green and somewhat bamboo-like with fans of evergreen leaves at the top. They are less hardy, although *I. japonica* (AGM), often sold as 'Ledger's Variety', is said to be hardier and can be grown outside in sunny spots where winters are not too cold. This species has horizontal green rhizomes plus stems, up to 100cm (39in), often shorter, and very orchid-like falls, with all parts of the flower prettily fringed. *I. japonica* 'Variegata' (AGM), also sold as 'Aphrodite', has leaves striped with pale cream and flowers less readily in cooler areas. 'Bourne Graceful', a hybrid between 'Ledger's Variety' and another form of *I. japonica,* has very pale mauve flowers. Good soil, and mulching with rich compost, are needed, and all forms do well in pots.

I. confusa (AGM) is noticeably less hardy and safer under glass, but it can be tried outside in warm, dry parts of Britain in frost-

The flowers of Evansia (crested) Iris japonica *are often mistaken for orchids. With many buds on a stem, it blooms for some weeks.*

free and very well-drained sites. It has tall green canes, 30–80cm (12–32in) long, bearing large fans of leaves and branched stems of frilly white flowers with orange-yellow crests and fall markings. A collected form, 'Martyn Rix', has pretty blue-violet flowers and seems to be hardier but dislikes direct sun.

UNGUICULARES IRISES

I. unguicularis (AGM) can be one of the most rewarding plants in the garden, or one of the most frustrating. Its clumps of lavender-blue blooms in a mild spell in the depths of winter are a lovely and cheering sight, as is the succession of flowers from late autumn through to spring. The frustration comes when given ideal conditions – alkaline, very well-drained soil, in full sun, with a wall at its back for extra warmth – its blooming is still sparse or fails to happen at all. Next door's garden may have a plant doing wonderfully; it could even be one you gave away… There is no simple reason for this: it might be that heavy feeding has produced leaves at the expense of flowers

and the extra foliage has shaded the rhizomes, or they may not have had enough sun if the summer is cool and damp. Even when flowers do appear, slugs and snails may find them first, or birds peck the flowers to find nectar. The stem is tiny, the ovary only just above the rhizome, with the flower at the top of the 15–20cm (6–8in) perianth tube. The best way to enjoy the flowers and their scent is to pull the tubes gently from their base and take them indoors: buds will open in water.

Make flowering more likely by digging in a little general fertilizer, not too high in nitrogen, before planting, and ensuring that divisions are of a fair size – small pieces are hard to establish. Plant the rhizomes at the soil surface. Some plants do well in rock gardens, or by spreading into gravel paths. If sun is in short supply, trim back the long, evergreen leaves to 15cm (6in) or so in summer; dead ones should be gently pulled away at any time.

'Walter Butt' is one of the most heavily scented cultivars and often begins to bloom early, with large flowers of silvery pale lilac; 'Marondera' is an extra-vigorous clone with typical flowers, and the narrow-leaved 'Mary Barnard' AGM is deep purple and usually free-flowering. Other narrow-leaved variants such as subsp. *cretensis*, subsp. *carica* var. *angustifolia* and 'Abington Purple' may need more shelter and even overhead protection in wet winters. White forms vary in vigour and flower quality. There are pink-flowered cultivars and several with flowers variegated in white, lavender and purple.

I. lazica (AGM) has a similar habit and flowering season to *I. unguicularis* but grows in dampish, rather shady places near the Black Sea. It is a rewarding plant for cooler gardens and deserves to be better known. It has quite broad, bright green leaves and flowers of lavender to dark purple. 'Joy Bishop' is redder in tone.

Winter's reward – a wonderful clump of Iris unguicularis *with flowers almost entirely hiding the leaves.*

PACIFIC COAST IRISES

Native to Oregon and Washington, as well as northern California, Pacific Coast irises (Series Californicae) are often also called Californians. Most grow in mountainous, forested areas, usually near the edges of woodland where there is some light; *I douglasiana* (AGM) occurs near the coast or a little way

inland in open situations. A few species are not reliably hardy in Britain and, as most are evergreen, they will not withstand very cold continental-type winters. They have small woody rhizomes with grassy leaves, and flower in late spring in a wide range of colours, the cultivars usually having beautifully patterned falls and signals – jewel-like is an apt description.

'Roaring Camp' is an example of the vivid colouring and patterns that occur in Pacific Coast irises, which are easily grown from seed.

I. douglasiana tolerates a little lime, otherwise acid or neutral soil is essential for all Pacific Coast irises, and it should be high in humus – leafmould, if not alkaline, is very good. Division and transplanting should be done in early autumn when the roots must not be allowed to get dry; if necessary, stand the plants in shallow water temporarily, or wrap the roots in sphagnum moss, which can be left around them when they are planted. Plant the rhizomes about 2.5cm (1in) deep and provide a light mulch of good compost or leafmould. In warmer places, they enjoy semi-shade but need more sun in cooler gardens, if they are to flower, however, they should never get too dry in summer. Keep new plants well watered until they are growing away but do not use alkaline water.

PCIs make excellent groundcover around shrubs, especially ericaceous ones such as rhododendrons, or among perennials that grow taller after the irises have flowered and provide shade. They can be grown in pots, an advantage if garden conditions are unsuitable, but do not let them get pot-bound. As cut flowers, in smaller-scale arrangements, the subtlety of their design can be seen at close quarters.

I. douglasiana, I. innominata and *I. tenax* are most often seen in gardens. The first has three to nine flowers on rather lax branched stems up to 70cm (28in) long; lavender shades are most common although the colour range includes red-purple through to cream and white. The evergreen leaves are relatively wide and long, perhaps with red bases. Also evergreen is *I. innominata* with finer, shorter, dark green leaves and one or two flowers on each upright stem, 15–25cm (6–10in) high. A colourful species, it is most commonly yellow with pretty veining, but can be cream, orange, blue, lilac or purple. *I. tenax* is similar in size to *I. innominata*, with

The stems of diminutive Pacific Coast species Iris tenax splay outwards from the centre of the plant.

purple, lavender or creamy yellow flowers and leaves that can die back in winter. *I. thompsonii* is also a similar size in blue or purple. Scented flowers, sometimes close to true blue, are a feature of *I. macrosiphon,* which is evergreen. Small leaves are produced on the stems of *I. bracteata,* yellow-flowered, and *I. purdyi,* cream-flowered with pink or purple veins; both 20–30cm (8–12in) tall. The bluest flowers are found in *I. munzii,* but this is quite tender.

Where the species grow together they readily hybridize, and breeders have worked over the last 50 years to produce cultivars in all the species' colours and more, usually with broader petals and heavier substance. These can be bought as named clones – if possible, choose container-grown specimens, as the roots of imported plants must be washed clean of soil and they do not always survive, despite being carefully packed. Seed of mixed hybrids should give a variety of colours. Space the seed well apart in pots of lime-free compost, cover lightly with compost or grit and plunge the pots in an open frame or shaded place until the seedlings have five leaves each, then plant out in their permanent positions in spring or early autumn. Disturb the roots as little as possible and keep the plants nicely moist until they are well established.

British-bred 'No Name' (AGM), bright yellow and looking like a large *I. innominata* (hence the name), is the only PCI to have a Dykes Medal. 'Banbury Beauty' (AGM), lavender with a purple signal, and other cultivars with the 'Banbury' prefix are all recommended.

Recommended varieties

'Agnes James' AGM A white form of *I. douglasiana.* Height 25cm (10in).
'Arnold Sunrise' AGM White, shaded blue; pale orange fall centres. Height 25cm (10in).
'Big Money' AGM Mid- to dark yellow. Height 30cm (12in).
'Blue Ballerina' AGM Near white with a black and purple signal. Height 38cm (15in).
'Broadleigh Carolyn' AGM Pale blue with deeper veining; purple signal. Height 45cm (18in). Also other 'Broadleigh' cultivars.
'Goring Ace' AGM Gold with crimson veins and edge. Height 25cm (10in).

'**Little Tilgates**' AGM Peach self with a radiant centre. Height 30cm (12in).

Cal-sibs

These are hybrids between PCIs and Sino-Siberians (p.52). Amos Perry, a legend among plant breeders, crossed *I. chrysographes* and *I. douglasiana* to produce 'Margot Holmes', a red-purple, which won the first ever British Dykes Medal in 1927 and is still available. Modern hybrids include 'Fine Line' (AGM), pale yellow veined, with purple giving a cinnamon-pink effect, 48cm (19in) high; 'Golden Waves' (AGM), light yellow, 60cm (24in) high; 'Wise Gift' AGM, deep violet, 56cm (22in) tall. These are sterile diploids, although tetraploids, which should be fertile, have been induced in this group, as with the Siberian irises (see below). 'Goring Steeple' (AGM) has yellow standards and style arms and magenta-rose falls, veined purple, 70cm (28in) tall. Others are on trial.

SIBERIAN IRISES

Siberian irises are generally very easy-going garden plants, needing a humus-rich soil that does not get too dry for too long, although established plants can withstand drought fairly well. They dislike being waterlogged. Planting and division are best done soon after flowering ends, but can be delayed until early autumn, especially if the irises are planted with other perennials with whom they associate well. Use plenty of well-rotted manure or compost, perhaps adding some slow-release fertilizer, and plant about 5cm (2in) deep. The divisions should have three to four rhizomes each. Water well on replanting, and later as necessary. Mulching to replenish food supplies and conserve moisture is beneficial. Open, fairly sunny situations are best for flowering.

I. sibirica (AGM) is not native to Siberia, but grows further west, from Russia to central Europe. It has two close relatives: *I. sanguinea* (formerly *I. orientalis*) (AGM) does inhabit parts of Siberia as well as countries in the Far East, and *I. typhifolia,* is native to China and has only recently been brought into cultivation in Europe and the USA. Even if it is only partly correct, Siberian rises is a convenient title for Series Sibiricae species and cultivars.

Long popular in gardens, *I. sibirica* has narrow, green deciduous leaves, like all plants in this group. Its branched stems, 90cm (36in) or taller, carry up to ten smallish, fluttering violet-blue and white flowers. *I. sanguinea* is shorter in leaf and stem, around 75cm (30in) high, with larger, dark violet flowers, two to a stem. The spathes covering the ovaries are reddish; they are green in 'Alba'. (They are also green in *I. sibirica*, going brown and papery later.) There is some confusion between the white forms of these species, not

A white Siberian iris demonstrates how well they combine with other plants, here with Digitalis purpurea *f.* albiflora *and a white* Potentilla fruticosa.

helped by their readiness to interbreed.

Only since botanists were able to revisit China in the late 20th century has *I. typhifolia* been found to be closely related to the other species. Its stems are usually shorter than those of *I. sibirica*, and it has narrower leaves. The blue-violet flowers are slightly larger with no prominent signal, although this seems somewhat variable. It flowers earlier than the other species, beginning in late spring, and may like damper soil but flower less well in cooler areas.

I. sibirica and *I. sanguinea* are the ancestors of most cultivars currently available; *I. typhifolia* is being added to the mix for its earlier flowering and because it quite often reblooms. There are many named Siberians in all shades of blue, violet, purple, lavender, wine-red and white. Yellow and lavender-pink varieties have been developed and blended with blues and reds for an even wider colour range. Flower form is less vertical – falls mostly arch or flare – and there may be feathering (fimbriation) on the style arms where several colours are often blended; signals can be gold or white and falls may have narrow edges of these colours. There are a few dwarf cultivars, including 'Baby Sister', only 15–23cm (6–9in) tall but with relatively large, mid-blue flowers, and dark violet 'Annick', 30cm (12in) tall, as well as dwarf forms   blue-violet or white – of the two main species.

Tetraploid cultivars, with twice the normal number of chromosomes, were induced by treatment with colchicine, then interbred to develop the race. They have stronger substance in leaves and flowers and may be more vigorous than diploids, although growing no taller. One of the earliest, 'Silver Edge' (AGM), a blue bitone with white fall edges, is rightly popular and others are widely available.

Repeat flowering tends to happen three to four weeks after the first bloom period, although some rebloom later. *I. typhifolia* and a number of cultivars show this trait, although the right conditions are needed – sufficient moisture and adequate but not excessive heat. 'Soft Blue' (AGM), 75cm (30in) tall, and the slightly shorter, violet 'Reprise' (AGM), have both proved to repeat reliably in the Wisley trial, as has the violet-blue tetraploid 'Exuberant Encore', which has short stems in May and June but taller, better branched ones in June and July.

Virtually all Siberian irises can be recommended as good garden plants. Many older cultivars are still popular, even if they do not quite compare with modern ones for colour and size of bloom. 'Perry's Blue', 'Helen Astor' (light red), 'Mrs Rowe' (pale lilac), 'Papillon' (pale blue), and 'Caesar's Brother' (dark violet), are well worth growing as are 'White Swirl' (AGM) and light violet-blue 'Cambridge' (AGM), a British Dykes medallist.

Recommended varieties

(T) indicates tetraploid

'Berlin Ruffles' AGM (T) Ruffled medium blue. Height 100cm (39in). British/European Dykes Medal.

'Butter and Sugar' AGM White standards; yellow falls. Flowers less well in cool conditions. Height 68cm (27in). Morgan-Wood Medal (AIS).

'Dreaming Yellow' AGM White to creamy yellow. May rebloom. Height 90cm (36in).

'Glaslyn' AGM (T) Pale blue standards; darker falls. Height 98cm (38in).

'Harpswell Happiness' AGM (T) White self with yellow-green veins. Height 75cm (30in).

'Lady Vanessa' Wine-red bitone. Height 90cm (36in). Morgan-Wood Medal.

'Rosselline' shows one of the newer combinations of colours in Siberian irises.

Siberian irises, such as 'Butter and Sugar', can be grown in almost any garden where conditions are not very dry.

'Perfect Vision' AGM (T) Blue bitone with turquoise style arms. Height 80cm (32in) British DM.

'Pink Haze' Pale lavender-pink standards; deeper falls. Height 88cm (35in). Morgan-Wood Medal.

'Plissée' AGM (T) Ruffled deep blue; falls edged white. Height 88cm (35in).

'Roisin' AGM Lavender-pink bitone. Height 90cm (36in).

'Rosselline' AGM Standards lilac; falls red-violet. Height 65cm (26in).

'Ruffled Velvet' AGM Red-purple; gold signal. Height 75cm (30in). Morgan Award (AIS).

'Shirley Pope' AGM Very dark red-purple, velvety falls; white signal. Height 80cm (32in).

SINO-SIBERIAN IRISES

The name Sino-Siberian has been adopted for species and cultivars in the Chrysographes group, which botanists include in Series Sibiricae. Although closely related to the Siberians, they have a different chromosome number and do not naturally hybridize with them.

The species are found in China and westwards to the Himalayas. Although fairly easy to grow, they prefer damper, but not boggy, and more acid conditions than the Siberians. The flowers are smaller, while the colour range is wider as yellow occurs naturally in addition to blue, purple and reddish shades. Signal areas, and often all parts in cultivars, are prettily marked. Although some plants are long lived, this group can flourish for a while and then decline for no obvious reason; good cultivation, as for Siberians, will help to keep them going. They are easy to grow from seed, but interbreed very readily so it can be difficult to get true species.

I. chrysographes (AGM), which lends its name to the whole group, is usually blue-purple, but quite variable, with gold lines in the signal area, the 'gold writing' of its name. There are black forms, which may lack the signal, and 'Rubella' is deep wine-red. The stems, which produce two flowers, are around 35cm (14in) tall; the leaves are slender and grassy. *I. delavayi* (AGM) is altogether huskier, and can grow up to 1.5m (5ft), with quite large, dark violet flowers on branched stems. *I. clarkei* (AGM),

In moist, slightly acid soil, Iris chrysographes *'Black Knight' produces some of the darkest flowers in nature.*

60cm (24in) high, has pretty blue-violet to reddish-violet flowers with white signals, two per stem, while *I. bulleyana* is similar in size to *I. chrysographes* with blue-violet flowers, and a white form. *I. dykesii* is probably a hybrid; plants named as this can be very variable. The yellow species are *I. forrestii* 15–40cm (6–16in) tall, with leaves glossy green above, greyish underneath and *I. wilsonii* which is more vigorous, growing to 60–75cm (24–30in) tall, and slightly paler yellow; neither is branched.

Seed of mixed hybrids, from specialist societies, should give a variety of interesting flowers. Some popular cultivars include 'Mandarin Purple', 85cm (34in) tall; 'Blue Meadow Fly' ('Blaue Wiesenmotte'), dark blue violet with white signals and style arms; and 'Gelbe Mantel', a tall plant with yellow flowers. Further hybridizing is going on in the USA and Germany with very interesting results.

IRIS SETOSA (AGM)

This hardy species grows almost as far north as the Arctic Circle in North America, mainly in Labrador and Alaska, and in eastern Asia from Siberia into northern China and Japan. The standards are often mere bristles, only the style arms and the falls being noticeable. There are red-purple and blue-purple and intermediate colour forms, including lavender-pink, and good whites 'Alba' and 'Kosho-En', the latter with dark spathes setting off the flowers. Heights go from 30–90cm (12–36in) with taller plants having elegant branching and numerous buds; 'Hondoensis' is one such, with velvety purple flowers. There is also a rare form with variegated leaves.

These are easy irises to grow, planted 2.5–5cm

Iris hookeri, a charming dwarf relative of I. setosa, *may have enlarged standards.*

This Tetra-Sibtosa seedling, a tetraploid hybrid between the Chrysographes Series and Iris setosa, carries its flowers high above its leaves.

(1¼–2in) deep in neutral to mildly acid, moisture-retentive but not waterlogged soil, in sun or part shade. The fairly wide leaves are deciduous.

I. hookeri is dwarf, about 15cm (6in) tall, with slate-blue flowers, which sometimes have standards as large as the falls and lying over them. It has been given species status very recently and may still be found labelled *I. setosa* var. *canadensis*, *I. setosa* 'Nana', or *I. setosa* var. *arctica*, which is quite different. A moist spot in the rock garden suits it well.

Series Tripetalae has one other member, *I. tridentata* from the south-eastern USA. It is not reliably hardy in most parts of Britain but could succeed under glass.

Hybrids from Siberian irises and *I. setosa* give well-branched plants with plenty of flowers that tend towards the form of the Siberians and are good in the garden. Diploids are sterile, but fertile tetraploids have been achieved using colchicine. Sibtosas, as they are called, are available in Germany and the USA, and should be offered in Britain before long.

IRIS FOETIDISSIMA (AGM)

One of the two British natives (the other is *I. pseudacorus*, p.61), this is a European and North African species, valued in the garden for its colourful seeds, which stay attached to their pods all winter, and as a foliage plant, although the flowers are not to be despised. It is also known as the gladwyn, gladdon or stinking iris because the leaves smell unpleasant, albeit briefly, if cut or bruised. It will grow almost anywhere, except in water, and even survives in dry shade under trees, although it is more rewarding if treated better.

In plantings of perennials or among (but not overwhelmed by) shrubs, with reasonably good soil, the glossy evergreen leaves catch the light. The usual mauve and brown flowers are not eyecatching, but there are bluer forms; 'Moonshy' and the

The seeds of Iris foetidissima *stay attached to the pods until spring, and stems can be cut and hung upside-down to dry for winter arrangements.*

Evergreen Iris foetidissima *'Variegata' has valuable foliage all year round, often more widely striped than it is here.*

two varieties *citrina* and *lutescens* have yellow flowers. Four to seven, or sometimes more flowers are borne on short branches on upright stems, 35–45cm (14–18in) tall, in midsummer, to be followed by pods, which split open in autumn to reveal red, orange or yellow seeds, white in 'Fructo Albo'. 'Variegata' (AGM) has good foliage striped lengthwise in shades of green and white, but is less vigorous and less ready to flower and set seed. As with other beardless irises, it is easier to establish divisions that have several rhizomes in a small clump.

SPURIA IRISES

Widely distributed from Europe through Russia and Turkey to western China, the spuria irises come in heights from a

few centimetres to 2m (6ft) and do well in rock gardens or in
mixed plantings, but do need sun in order to flower well. They
extend the main flowering season to midsummer and later; the
little *I. graminea* (AGM), 15–20cm (6–8in) tall, is usually the
earliest with its purple flowers smelling of plums or greengages.
Its variant *pseudocyperus* is taller and just as pretty but without
the scent. *I. sintenisii* (AGM) is a little shorter and has white
flowers very heavily veined with deep violet.

For planting at the front of borders rather than in the rock
garden there are several species. *I. kerneriana* (AGM) has pale
yellow flowers on stems of 20–40cm (8–16in), with nectar that
is very attractive to ants. *I. spuria* subsp. *maritima* is deep violet-
blue with paler falls, and variably marked style arms (these are
very prominent in the spurias, lying over the long hafts of the
falls which end in nearly circular blades, often with signal
patches). In subsp. *sogdiana* the flowers are pale blue to lilac and
subsp. *spuria* is violet-blue. These last two are up to 50cm (20in)
in height. Two for planting a little further back are subsp.
halophila, which reaches 40–90cm (16–36in) and has creamy
yellow flowers, and subsp. *carthaliniae*, 90–100cm (36–39in) and
sky blue. A brighter deeper blue is produced by subsp. *notha*,
which also has a white form, and subsp. *musulmanica*, both of
similar stature. Generally taller still are *I. orientalis* (formerly *I.*
ochroleuca), white with a
yellow signal on the falls,
and *I. monnieri*, soft yellow,
both being around 100cm
(39in). *I. crocea* (AGM) (syn.
I. aurea), golden yellow, can
be 90–150cm (3–5ft).

While the smaller spurias
have two flowers per stem,
the number increases with
the height of the plant and
can be as many as nine in *I.*
crocea. A sizeable clump of a
tall spuria iris is a striking
sight in flower, and after that
the stiff upright leaves

*'Protégé' shows the
distinctive flower
shape of the taller
spuria irises.*

provide height and contrast with rounder plant shapes.

The larger spurias need nourishment as well as sun to produce their flower stems and increase for future years, so should be planted in good soil, mildly acid to mildly alkaline, with rotted manure or a general fertilizer incorporated; humus is desirable to retain moisture, but allow drainage, and the rhizomes should be set about 5cm (2in) deep.

Old hybrids that stand comparison with newer cultivars are 'Ochraurea' and 'Shelford Giant' (AGM) with yellow flowers – the latter often reaching 2m (6ft) or more tall – and 'Monspur Cambridge Blue' (AGM). These grow and flower well in Britain. Many modern cultivars have been bred in the USA and may not bloom too well in Britain's cooler summers, although some have gained AGMs and more may do so after trial.

Recommended varieties

'Belise' AGM Lavender-blue. Height 94cm (37in).

'Cherokee Lace' Yellow with brown veining. Height 100cm (39in). British bred.

'Clarke Cosgrove' AGM Lavender with a small yellow signal. Height 98cm (38in). Nies Award (AIS).

'Dawn Candle' Standards white; falls yellow; signal orange. Height 1.2m (4ft). Nies Award.

'Destination' AGM Yellow-orange self. Height 100cm (39in).

'Ila Crawford' AGM White, orange signal. Height 91cm (36in).

'Janice Chesnik' Ruffled tawny gold self. Height 1.2–1.5m (4–6ft). Nies Award.

'Marilyn Holloway' Standards pale lavender; falls yellow, edged lavender. Height 98cm (38in).

'Missouri Rivers' Ruffled blue with a yellow signal. Height 98cm (38in). Nies Medal (AIS).

'Protégé' AGM Blue standards; white falls veined blue. Height 90cm (36in).

LOUISIANA IRISES

These are the irises in Series Hexagonae, and in fact are found across the southern USA, from Florida and the Carolinas to Texas. The hardier species, such as *I. fulva* and *I. brevicaulis*, grow as far north as Missouri and some Midwest states, and they will survive in warmer parts of Britain. *I. fulva* has coppery orange flowers and *I. brevicaulis* has a zigzag stem 15–30cm (6–12in) long bearing lovely blue flowers. The hybrid between them, *I.* x *fulvala* (AGM), has vivid purple flowers, is very robust and needs damper soil than its parents, such as a bog. All can be set back if their evergreen leaves are damaged in winter and need as much sun as possible with the rhizomes at or just below the soil surface.

In the USA there are cultivars in many colours. Louisianas do well in much of the North Island of New Zealand, and are particularly good in Australia, where cultivars raised in New South Wales have won a series of Dykes Medals. 'Clyde Redmond' is one that has done well in a fairly warm British garden, with bright blue flowers in late June. Other modern cultivars will usually flower in Britain if grown in large pots (they are vigorous plants, which spread widely) standing in water, under glass. The problem is not so much with growing them as getting them to flower.

The moderate height and elegant flowers of I. kerneriana, a spuria iris, make it a useful border plant.

Louisiana irises need warmth to flower but Iris x fulvala will bloom outside in southern Britain, or in a cool greenhouse.

MOISTURE-LOVING IRISES

One of the loveliest irises is *I. laevigata* (AGM) in its typical violet-blue form. Although all the species, hybrids and cultivars in this group – Series Laevigatae – need moisture to grow well, many are satisfied with soil, high in humus and staying reasonably damp in summer but generally not alkaline; *I. laevigata* and its offspring are the only ones that really need to grow in shallow water at the edge of a pool, planted in 30cm (12in) or so of soil enriched with manure and with 5–8cm (2–3in) of water covering the rhizomes. Its 45cm (18in) stems have two to four flowers, appearing in the later part of the main season.

Iris laevigata *has one of the loveliest iris flowers, and does best when grown in shallow water.*

The standards of *I. laevigata* are fairly small and upright but in cultivars they can be taller and wider and may lie between the falls producing 'double' varieties. Its cultivars 'Alba' and 'Weymouth Purity' are white, 'Snowdrift' is a double white; all of these are touched with pale violet. Some white flowers are more marked with violet-blue – this is pale in 'Weymouth Elegant' and very dark in the double 'Colchesterensis'. 'Atropurpurea' is a deep wine-purple, 'Regal' lighter wine-red; 'Lilacina' is a pale blue double, with a darker centre. Very striking is 'Weymouth Midnight', a double, very deep violet with contrasting white central stripes occuring on each petal. 'Variegata' (AGM) has slightly paler blue flowers than the type, which are set off beautifully by foliage striped in green and white that lasts for the entire summer.

Iris pseudacorus (AGM)

While no garden pond should be without at least one of the Laevigatae (they increase steadily but not too rapidly for even a small pool), the same cannot be said of the British native yellow flag, *I. pseudacorus*, which is really too vigorous for all but very large ponds or lakes. It will grow at the edges of slow-flowing streams and, when well rooted, may cope with temporary faster flows after rain. In drier places it is less vigorous and a useful addition to groups of perennials, as are its cultivars 'Variegata' (AGM), with its lovely spring foliage striped in shades of yellow and green, and 'Lime Sorbet' with pale greenish-yellow leaves. Both gradually become all-green from midsummer and have shorter flowering stems – around 75cm (30in) – compared to the typical form and some others, which can reach from 80–166cm (32–66in). 'Esk' and 'Sun in Splendour' are particularly tall, even when not in water. 'Golden Queen' is shorter and, like 'Sun in Splendour', has large flowers.

'Alba' is palest cream with purplish lines around the pale yellow signal. Pale yellows have names such as 'Cream', 'Ivory', or 'Turnipseed', which originated in an American nursery of that name; var. *bastardii* is lemon yellow. 'Beuron' and 'Ilgengold' are tetraploids, sturdier in build, the latter a bitone with pale standards. 'Sun Cascade' and 'Flore Pleno' are doubles, one flower growing from the centre of another. Flowers of dwarf forms, 50–70cm (20–28in) tall, can be rather hidden by the foliage, and fewer than the normal complement of up to twelve.

'Holden Clough' (AGM), 60–90cm (24–36in) tall, has much brown veining on its yellow ground and is of somewhat mysterious origin. It may be a sport of *I. pseudacorus* or a hybrid with another species. It is the parent of some good irises: 'Roy Davidson' AGM is bright yellow, lightly

Iris pseudacorus needs space, beside water or in it. It is well known, but should not be undervalued because of this.

veined with chestnut brown on the falls, the signal sharply edged in brown; 'Berlin Tiger' AGM has intense brown fall veining; 'Phil Edinger' AGM is densely veined including the standards and style crests, and has a brown signal.

Iris versicolor and *Iris virginica*

I. pseudacorus is widespread in the wild, throughout Europe and right across Asia to Japan, but is not found in North America, which has instead the blue flag, *I. versicolor* (AGM), which is found from eastern Canada southwards to Texas, and its close relation *I. virginica*, which occurs in south-eastern USA. The first is an excellent garden plant, and it will grow in water or any soil not too dry or very acid or alkaline. Its well-branched stems, 25–60cm (10–24in) or more tall (they are taller when grown in water), have up to seven flowers, usually violet-blue but with natural colour variants including white, pink in var. *rosea*, wine-red in 'Kermesina', and purple. Among its cultivars are bicolors such as 'Party Line' in light and darker pink with white styles or pale ground colours with deeper veins – for example 'Between the Lines', white veined with blue, and 'Mint Fresh' with red veining – which sometimes merge at the petal ends into solid colour, violet in 'Whodunit'. Other variations can be seen in the 'Rowden' series of cultivars. The most dramatic is 'Mysterious Monique'; this has velvety, deep red-purple falls with large gold and white signals, wine-red standards and white style arms marked with red.

    I. virginica has leafy, unbranched stems of up to 90cm (36in) and paler flowers – lavender to violet – than *I. versicolor*. It is not as hardy, although var. *shrevei*, which is branched and scented, can be grown in Britain and some new cultivars may be hardier.

    I. x robusta is a name for hardy hybrids between *I. versicolor* and *I. virginica*. 'Gerald Darby' (AGM) has dark purple stems with violet-blue flowers, the foliage stained purple at its base; and 'Dark Aura' is darker still with deep purple blooms on black stems and beetroot-red spring foliage, which goes green later. 'Nutfield Blue' and 'Mountain Brook' are blue-violet, the second a deeper shade than the first.

Hybrids

Hybridizers have been crossing species of the Laevigatae with good results. *I. pseudacorus* with *I. versicolor* has yielded tall hybrids with violet veins on white grounds and yellow signals, as in 'Limbo'. The veining is red-purple in 'Appointer', while the shorter 'Regal Surprise' has light reddish-violet standards, cream style arms and red-violet falls with yellow signals.

I. pseudacorus has also been crossed with *I. ensata* (p.64), first in Japan where 'Aichi-no-Kagayaki' and 'Kinboshi' were produced. They have yellowish foliage and are not very vigorous. Green-leaved and more robust, with bold yellow flowers, is the fertile hybrid 'Chance Beauty'. Its falls are flaring and lightly veined with red-brown around yellow signals outlined in darker brown. Seedlings appear to be pure *I. pseudacorus* and if allowed to fall into the clump may take over, so it should be dead-headed promptly or the seeds carefully collected. More of these hybrids are being developed in Japan (see below).

The interspecies hybrid 'Regal Surprise', I. pseudacorus × I. *versicolor, is a good plant for moist soil.*

Canadian-bred hybrids of *I. versicolor* and *I. ensata*, Versatas, are making available more irises for damp places. Current trials of moisture-loving irises (Wisley in 2003–2005) include two Versatas. 'Enfant Prodige' has lilac standards, large deeper lilac falls with yellow signals haloed in deep violet, and white styles. Well branched with numerous buds it is 1.1m (3½ft) tall. 'Violet Minuet', a little shorter, has velvety falls with clear yellow signals. The trial also has 'Starting Versi-Laev' and other hybrids between *I. versicolor* and *I. laevigata*, plus Sibcolor hybrids, Siberian cultivars crossed with *I. versicolor*.

JAPANESE IRISES

These also belong to Series Laevigatae (see Moisture-loving irises, p.60) and have been collected, cultivated and bred in Japan for centuries, although the species *I. ensata* (AGM) (often called *I. kaempferi*) is native to northern China and eastern Siberia, as well as Japan. The spectacular mass plantings of cultivars that are flooded at flowering time have led to the idea that Japanese cultivars must be grown in permanent water, which is not the case. While they can be planted at the edge of a natural pond or one of puddled clay, they are also happy in a peaty bog or an acid garden soil that does not dry out and is enriched with composted farmyard manure. What must be emphasized is the need for acidity – in the soil and any water used on them. A very few will tolerate slight alkalinity, but the majority react very quickly to it with yellowing leaves and poor growth and they will die if left alone. Where the garden soil is unsuitable, pot culture in ericaceous compost with added manure, or a plastic-lined bed into which ground water cannot penetrate, can be tried.

I. ensata, the original species, has narrow upright standards

'Berlin Tiger' is an excellent iris for moist soil, with very striking flowers.

and broad, hanging falls in dark red-purple and there are purple-blue, pink-and-white and white variants. Collected from the wild in Japan and grown in gardens, especially around shrines, these were named Nagai types after the region where they were found. Cross-pollination by insects led to other types evolving. Those with horizontal falls were named after the Edo (Tokyo) region where the gardens were often viewed from raised platforms so the flatter form showed the flowers better. Ise irises with papery pendent falls were used for pot culture while the robust Higo strain, evolved from Edo irises, provided the ancestors of modern cultivars bred in Japan, the USA and elsewhere. The Japanese name for the cultivars is Hanashobu.

The colours remain broadly the same although there are a wide range of tones, but patterns and flower forms have changed considerably. 'Double' or 'six-fall' cultivars have enlarged standards lying on the same horizontal or arching level as the falls, while in multiple petal or 'peony-flowered' irises, the

Iris ensata from the Tokyo region is an ancestor of cultivars developed in Japan over several centuries.

style arms have become much larger and more petaloid. Not all cultivars have branching stems like the species, but heights are similar – mainly 60–90cm (24–36in). The green leaves have a prominent midrib; they are grey-green with white stripes in 'Variegata' (AGM).

Tetraploids have been developed in the USA and so have repeat-blooming cultivars, but their performance in Britain's climate is, so far, rather patchy; they do much better in areas that have warmer summers. Extra feeding and adequate water are needed to encourage rebloom.

In Japan, striking hybrids between *I. pseudacorus* and *I. ensata* called Pseudata or 'Eye Shadow' irises are being bred, following on from earlier work on such hybrids (see p.63). They have green foliage and are vigorous; pictures show them to have clearly edged signals on falls coloured from white and yellow through near-orange, bronze, pink to violet, veined or plain, sometimes combining several colours. Clearly, they are highly desirable plants.

Recommended varieties of *I. ensata*

SINGLE (3-FALL):

'**Alba**' White self. Height 75cm (30in).

'**Barr Purple East**' AGM Purple-violet bitone, darker veins, yellow signal. Height 120cm (48in).

'**Imperial Magic**' AGM Standards lilac, edged white; falls white marked with purple. Height 1.15m (4¹/₂ft).

'**Returning Tide**' AGM Standards violet-blue; falls lighter. May rebloom. Height 1m (3ft). Payne Award (AIS).

'**Rose Queen**' AGM Rose-pink self. Height 98cm (38in).

'**Rowden King**' Standards deep red-purple; styles white; falls pinkish-mauve. Has shown an ability to tolerate lime. Height 90cm (36in).

'**Rowden Mikado**' Standards and styles deep purple and white; falls white overlaid purple, blue and mauve. Somewhat lime-tolerant. Height 90cm (36in).

'**The Great Mogul**' AGM Black-purple self. Height 1.1m (3¹/₂ft).

DOUBLE (6-FALL) OR WITH MORE PETALS:

'**Beni-tsubaki**' Rose-violet with white veins and style arms.

An 'Eye Shadow' or Pseudata iris, bred in Japan by crossing cultivars of Iris pseudacorus *and* I. ensata.

Height 68cm (27in).

'Caprician Butterfly' AGM Standards purple, edged white; falls white, veined purple, gold signal. Height 90cm (36in). Payne Medal (AIS).

'Continuing Pleasure' AGM Deep violet-purple. May rebloom. Height 98cm (38in).

'Flashing Koi' White with red-purple halo, veins and style arms. Height 90cm (36in).

'Hercule' Large, mid- to dark blue, veined deeper. Height 90cm (36in).

'Katy Mendez' AGM Mid-violet, darker veins, yellow signals. Height 70cm (28in).

'Kuma-funjin' Very deep purple-blue. Height 90cm (36in).

'Light at Dawn' White with narrow blue borders. Height 80cm (32in).

'Moonlight Waves' White self, greenish hafts, semi-double. Height 90cm (36in).

'Oriental Eyes' Light violet shading to grey-white, purple halo and veins. Height 90cm (36in). Payne Medal.

'Pink Frost' Light orchid-pink self. Height 1m (3ft).

'Summer Storm' AGM Dark purple, extra styles and petaloids. May rebloom. Height 1.1m (3½ft).

OTHER BEARDLESS SPECIES

A number of species are well worth a place in the garden, and some that have hitherto been rare or unknown in cultivation are becoming available. (More detailed information on siting and cultivation is available in *The Guide to Species: Irises*, see p.88.)

A limy soil, not too dry and in full sun, suits *I. missouriensis* (AGM), which now includes *I. longipetala*. From the Rocky Mountains of the USA, it has white flowers much veined with blue-purple to lilac, but is fairly variable and may appear self-

*'Caprician Butterfly'
is a 'double' or
six-fall Japanese iris
with much enlarged
standards.*

coloured. Its stems are 20–90cm (8–36in) tall and branched, and
the leaves are semi-evergreen, for which reason it is best to
divide and replant it immediately flowering ends – June in
Britain. 'Tol-long' (AGM) has pale violet, veined flowers.

I. lactea AGM (syn. *I. biglumis*), found from China to central
Asia, is rather similar in appearance to *I. missouriensis* above but
prefers better drained, limy soil and tolerates drought when
established. Do not let the roots dry out when it is moved. The
5–30cm (2–12in) tall stem is unbranched, the flowers blue-
violet to white, and fragrant. In the past, this species was called
I. ensata, and man-made hybrids between it and Sino-Siberian
cultivars – Chrysata irises – need the same conditions as the
Sino-Siberians.

Some attractive dwarf species include *I. ruthenica*, a European
to Far Eastern iris. Its variety *nana* is very tiny with stems from
2.5cm (1in) tall; other forms reach up to 20cm (8in). The
flowers are dark violet, the falls veined or dotted on a white
ground; var. *nana* can be lighter and var. *leucantha* is white. This
is a fairly easy species for a moderately rich, light, lime-free soil
in sun or partial shade in a rock garden or alpine house.

I. verna also needs acid soil and should not be allowed to dry
out in summer, although drainage should be good. It is quite
widespread in some eastern and central states of the USA but
not easy to keep in cultivation. Tiny stems carry pretty,

relatively large, light violet-blue flowers with orange lines, surrounded by white signals, on the falls.

Another North American native with rather spidery but pretty flowers in blue-violet, white, pink or with plicata markings is *I. prismatica*. Stoloniferous, it wanders around in acid, fairly moist but well-drained soil; wet winters on heavy clay are not to its liking. The stems are 30–80cm (12–32in) tall, the leaves fine and grassy.

Two species in Subgenus *Nepalensis* may be tried outside in sunny place, if they are kept consistently moist in the growing season, from mid-spring to mid-autumn, but are then kept dry, or lifted and stored in dry sand or peat, when the leaves die back after flowering. These conditions are easier to regulate under glass. *I. decora* and *I. collettii* have very short-lived, pale purple flowers on stems up to 5cm (2in) in *I. collettii*, 10–30cm (4–12in) in *I. decora*. Both have tiny rhizomes or growing points with fleshy roots, which should be handled very carefully.

Iris verna is a delightful woodland iris from North America but can be short-lived in gardens.

BULBOUS IRISES

Varying from very tiny to around 60cm (24in) tall, the first of these irises flowers late in winter, if the weather is kind, or early spring, and different sorts continue until late summer. Some are not hardy and are dealt with later (see p.83); the smallest, although able to cope with most conditions outdoors, are good for bulb frames, or pots that can be brought indoors.

The earliest to bloom are members of Subgenus *Hermodactyloides*, which comprises the Reticulata irises – gems for the rock garden, troughs or pots. Flowering in late spring is Subgenus *Xiphium*, containing the Dutch hybrids – staple of the florist's shop for many months and decorative in the garden – the more delicate Spanish irises and *Iris latifolia*, the robust English irises. In bloom between these groups, with some overlap at either end, is Subgenus *Scorpiris*, the Juno irises.

Most of the bulbous irises that are suitable for the garden need sun and good drainage, moisture from autumn through to spring, and a good baking in summer to build up reserves for blooming the following year. Feeding with bonemeal or a fertilizer high in potash once flowering has finished helps build up the parent bulb and the offsets around its base.

RETICULATA IRISES

Although *I. reticulata* (AGM) gives this group its name and is a parent of numerous hybrids, the earliest Reticulatas to bloom – often in January in Britain if winter is mild – are *I. histrioides* and its named forms, all with sizeable violet-blue flowers. The style arms and crests are very prominent and the falls have

'Clairette', one of the bulbous Reticulata irises, is good in a pot or a sunny dry place in the garden.

pretty white, yellow and dark violet markings. *I. reticulata*, dark violet with narrower parts, follows a little later along with hybrids or forms such as 'J.S. Dijt', wine-purple. 'George' (AGM) is an excellent hybrid between *I. histrioides* 'Major' and 'J.S. Dijt' with the flower size of the first and colour of the second, it is very robust and reliable when established. Other hybrids between *I. histrioides* and *I. reticulata* with flowers intermediate in size between their parents' include 'Harmony', sky-blue, and 'Violet Beauty', bitone.

I. reticulata and the closely related, pale blue and purple *I. bakeriana* are the parents of, among others, 'Clairette' with pale blue standards and dark blue falls and 'Jeannine', purple-violet. Heights are generally around 10–15cm (4–6in).

Bright lemon yellow *I. danfordiae* strikes a cheerful note with tiny bristles for standards and is only 5–8cm (2–3in) tall. After blooming the bulb usually splits into many tiny bulblets. If it is planted 25cm (10in) deep and fed heavily for at least three years, in light soil, the bulblets may eventually reach flowering size. The alternative is to rely on the expertise of professional growers and buy new bulbs each year, which are relatively cheap.

I. winogradowii is the other yellow-flowered species, paler in colour but with flowers the size of *I. histrioides*. It needs more moisture than other Reticulatas when in growth and also later as the bulbs should not be allowed to dry out completely. There are very good hybrids between this and *I. histrioides*. Robust growers needing dryish sunny positions, they are good in rock gardens or deep troughs. 'Katharine Hodgkin' (AGM) has pale yellow flowers marked with blue and is 8cm (3in) tall; 'Frank Elder' is bluer; 'Sheila Ann Germaney' more purple-blue and still rare.

Recommended varieties

'Edward' Bright dark blue, orange ridge on the falls, scented.
'Gordon' Blue standards, blue-purple falls with an orange ridge.
'Ida' Pale blue, yellow ridge.
'Natascha' Palest blue-white, orange blotch, less vigorous.
'Pauline' Deep purple-violet, white ridge.
'Springtime' Blue bicolor with darker falls, white ridge.

JUNO IRISES

Subgenus *Scorpiris* contains a large number of species with a few suitable for growing in sunny, very well-drained places, such as a rock garden or the top of a dry wall. Shelter is needed in colder places, and these irises may be better under cover. Other species are rare and often difficult to cultivate (see Irises under glass, p. 78).

As well as bulbs, Junos have fleshy roots used for storing food; if these are damaged or lost the result is almost always the death of the bulb. The best way to buy them is as potted bulbs in growth. Handle them with care if they are bare-rooted and when replanting. The stem has a series of leaves growing up it and can resemble a small maize plant. In addition to terminal buds, there are others growing from one or more leaf joints (axils). The flowers are mostly quite sizeable with tiny downturned standards and very prominent style arms and crests, the falls usually with a central ridge or crest on their upper part.

I. bucharica (AGM) is hardy in many places and easy to grow. Its stems up to 40cm (16in) tall have glossy green leaves and as many as six white flowers with yellow falls. An all-yellow form

Iris bucharica, *one of the easiest Juno irises to grow, has buds in each of the upper leaf axils.*

may still be found labelled, incorrectly, *I. orchioides* (the true species is less hardy). Other Junos that can be grown outside are: *I. graeberiana* with lavender flowers and a white area on the falls around the white ridge, or with yellow falls; *I. cycloglossa* with handsome lavender flowers and semi-erect standards on 20–40cm (8–16in) stems; *I. magnifica* (AGM), of similar height and pale lilac, and 'Alba' white with yellow around its white crest; *I. aucheri* (AGM), most often pale blue but varying from white to deep violet, up to 35cm (14in) and safest in well-sheltered spots; and *I. warleyensis* with bitone violet flowers and yellow crests, 20–40cm (8–16in) tall and also best in a sheltered spot. 'Sindpers' (AGM) is a hybrid from *I. aucheri* (formerly *I. sindjarensis*) crossed with the more tender *I. persica*. It is reasonably hardy with greenish-blue flowers on 25cm (10in) stems. Another hybrid for a warm dry spot is 'Warlsind' (*I. warleyensis* **x** *I. aucheri*), 25–35cm (10–14in) with yellow and blue flowers.

A Juno iris that is ideal for a bulb frame, as here, Iris cycloglossa *can also be grown in a warm spot outside, with very good drainage.*

XIPHIUM IRISES

The irises in this group are well known as cut flowers; the range offered by florists tends to be rather limited and growing your own gives a wider choice of colours, whether for cutting or not. Except for *I. latifolia*, they like similar positions to most bulbs – sunny and with good drainage – and when planted in autumn, 5cm (2in) deep, will reappear annually and increase with minimum care. Just gently fork in a little fertilizer (not manure) from time to time.

I. xiphium is known as the Spanish iris although it occurs in other countries around the western Mediterranean. It is slightly shorter and more slender than others of the subgenus, usually 40–60cm (16–24in) tall; its flowers are blue or violet, sometimes white. There are several variants: var. *battandieri* is white with orange on the falls, var. *lusitanica* is yellow, and var. *praecox* has large blue flowers and blooms earlier than the rest. Generally sold as mixed colours, they may include the named cultivars 'Cajanus' with yellow flowers, 'King of the Blues' with deep blue flowers with a yellow blotch, and 'Thunderbolt' with purple-brown standards and brown falls with a yellow blotch.

I. tingitana from North Africa has up to three flowers on stems 60cm (24in) tall but is less hardy than *I. xiphium*. The Dutch irises have been developed from hybrids between the two species and they come in shades and combinations of blue, violet, purple, bronze, orange, yellow and white. They flower soon after the Spanish irises – late spring to early summer – and for best results in the garden the largest bulbs obtainable should be planted, although some, for example 'Yellow Queen', do not make large bulbs. Those grown commercially for the cut-flower trade are usually grown from smaller bulbs that will only have one flower; two are normal for larger bulbs.

As with other bulbous irises, there is no trial of these irises at Wisley, but the excellent garden (and cut-flower) variety, dark violet-blue 'Professor Blaauw' has the AGM. Specialist bulb nurseries are the places to find other reliable cultivars including: 'Amber Beauty', yellow bitone; 'Apollo', tall and vigorous, palest blue and rich yellow; 'Blue Elegance', purple standards and blue falls; 'Bronze Queen', yellowish-brown; 'Cream Beauty', white standards and cream falls with yellow blotches;

'Duchy Blue', violet-blue bitone; 'Gipsy Beauty', blue standards, bronze falls; 'Lemon Queen', a bitone; 'Mauve King'; 'Oriental Beauty', blue standards and yellow falls and 'White Excelsior'.

I. latifolia (syn. *I. xiphioides*) (AGM) from north-west Spain and the Pyrenees needs to stay moister in summer than other bulbs but is otherwise very easy-going. The bold flowers are commonly dark violet-blue but red-purple, pale blue, lilac-pink and white are possible and a century ago all these were offered, often as a ground colour splashed with one or more others. The only survivor seems to be the very good white 'Mont Blanc' and for a long while only mixtures were available. Recently some named cultivars have appeared: 'Duchess of York', blue; 'Isabella', lilac-rose; 'King of the Blues', rich dark blue; 'Mansfield', wine-purple; and 'Mont Blanc' and 'Queen of the Blues' in pale blue. The bulbs are larger than those of the Dutch irises and should be planted about 8cm (3in) deep in good soil, in sun. The flowers are often flecked with darker markings, probably due to virus, but this does not seem to affect the vigour of the plants.

The shrub Cassinia leptophylla *subsp.* fulvida *makes a good background for* Iris latifolia *'Mont Blanc'.*

IRISES UNDER GLASS

There are very few irises that cannot tolerate any degree of frost – *I. speculatrix* from Hong Kong is one – but for some it is wet combined with cold that is fatal in the garden. A cold greenhouse, alpine house or bulb frame, where conditions can be controlled, is the place to grow these. Ventilation is important, so is watering, which must only be done at the right times and preferably from below: if it must be done from above, do not let water get into the foliage or rot will start. Use a free-draining compost such as JI No. 3 mixed with an equal quantity of grit (and magnesium limestone added for irises that need it), and top up with grit around the rhizomes or the necks of bulbs.

Some of the cane-type Evansias can be tried outside (see p.41) but may be safer in a bed or large pots in a cold greenhouse where they make big, handsome plants if well fed and not kept too dry. *I. confusa*, *I. japonica* and its cultivars, and 'Bourne Graceful' all appreciate this treatment. *I. wattii*, which has large, near-blue flowers, is not hardy in Britain. It grows up to 2m (6ft) and may need staking.

Irises that must be kept completely dry from the end of flowering until autumn and then be watered with care until spring may be grown in pots, but vigorous growers such as Arilbreds need space. The best place for them is a bulb frame, which is easily made by placing a cold frame on walls made from two courses of concrete blocks. Use the same compost mixture as above but add a low-nitrogen fertilizer.

The dramatic Oncocyclus irises are tempting but not easy where the atmosphere is damp, especially in summer; they need

Iris kolpakowskiana, an unusual bulbous iris of the Reticulata Group, is best grown under glass in Britain.

Tiny Juno Iris
nicolai *has several
colour forms and
must be grown
under glass.*

their own frame or a bed in an alpine house and ventilation is essential, as is an alkaline and very gritty compost. There is detailed advice in *The Guide to Species: Irises* (p.88). The large blooms of *I. gatesii* in white, cream or pinkish, veined and speckled brown or deep purple and with dark signals, are produced on 40cm (16in) stems; *I. iberica* and its subspecies are usually 20–30cm (8–12in) tall, with white flowers that are very closely veined, especially the falls. *I. sari*, yellowish with reddish to black veins, is 6–30cm (2½–12in); *I. barnumae* has several subspecies and forms, most are purple but f. *barnumae* is yellow and all are 10–25cm (4–10in) tall.

Some Regelias, Pseudoregelias and the Regelio-cyclus hybrids (see also p.36) are best grown under glass, in a frame where they have room to spread. These include the Regelia *I. korolkowii*, 20–30cm (8–12in) high with heavily veined pale flowers, and the Pseudoregelias *I. cuniculiformis*, lilac, and *I. narcissiflora*, yellow; *I. kemaonensis* with tiny stems and lilac-purple flowers with deeper blotches seems a little easier in Britain.

Although hardy Reticulatas are fine outside, growing them in deep pots or in a bulb frame protects the flowers, and in pots they can be brought indoors when in bloom. Species such as *I. hyrcana*, blue, *I. kolpakowskiana*, lilac-violet with darker falls, and *I. pamphylica*, blue and purple, are all less than 10cm (4in) high and safer in pots or a frame.

Tender bulbs in Subgenus *Xiphium* do best when grown in a bulb frame. *I. filifolia*, 25–45cm (10–18in) reddish-purple flowers with orange on the falls may be obtainable, as may *I. juncea* with yellow flowers.

Both hardy and less hardy Juno irises can be successfully grown in long-tom pots or in a frame; their storage roots need space and careful handling. Less hardy varieties include yellow *I. orchioides*, 30cm (12in) tall; violet and yellow *I. vicaria*, 35cm (14in) tall; and greenish-yellow *I. kopetdaghensis*, 25cm (10in) or more. *I. willmottiana* is 15cm (6in) tall and lavender flecked with blue, or white in 'Alba'; *I. narbutii*, a violet bitone with white crest, is only 8cm (3in) tall; and *I. nicolai*, 10cm (4in) tall, has several colour forms.

PROPAGATION AND HYBRIDIZING

DIVISION

Named cultivars must be propagated by division as they will not come true from seed; seedlings should never be given the parent's name, even if they look similar. Division and transplanting can be done with care any time between spring and autumn, but soon after flowering, when new increases and roots are appearing, is usually best. Pacific Coast irises are definitely better dealt with in early autumn.

Rhizomes develop growth buds at their sides, usually close to the main fan first, and these grow into rhizomes that increase in their turn. Allow small plants to grow until they can be used to make several divisions. Most irises should be divided into clumps with at least two to four rhizomes, but those that produce larger rhizomes, such as tall beardeds, can be split into single pieces. With those that may resent being disturbed, *I. unguicularis* and Pacific Coast irises for example, moving only half the plant at one time and leaving the rest *in situ* can insure you against total loss.

Cut large rhizomes cleanly at their junctions with others, and divide clumps with many small rhizomes, such as Siberians, by using the levering action of two forks back-to-back. Discard all dead material and also get rid of weak pieces, unless the iris is very special and you can give them extra care, such as in pots. Keep the roots of most beardless irises damp, especially PCIs, if they cannot be replanted immediately.

Bulblets at the base of iris bulbs can be left *in situ* to grow to flowering size or be lifted and grown on in a nursery bed.

Iris Innominata interplanted with hostas.

If a clump has weak leaves and no flowers, it needs lifting, dividing and replanting at the original depth with fertilizer added to the site.

Raising from seed

Iris seeds are comfortably large to handle and propagating plants this way is as easy as for most perennials. Seed can be sown in autumn or spring and it helps germination to soak it in tap water, changed daily, for 4–7 days. Cold treatment also seems to help – if seeds cannot be exposed to frost, they may be mixed with moist peat in a closed bag or container and left for three weeks in the refrigerator (not in the freezer).

Seeds can be sown in the open ground, but pots are safer. Use a good seed compost (lime-free for irises that need it) adding extra grit where good drainage is essential, space the seeds out and top with a thin layer of grit or compost. Keep the pots just moist – wet for water irises. Prick out the seedlings when they have three or four leaves or are about 15cm (6in) high; if they reach this stage in late summer, they may be safer in individual pots in a cold frame until spring. Space them 15–30cm (6–12in) apart, depending on the size they should attain, with the base of the leaves just below the soil surface, especially for bearded irises.

Rarely, an iris will bloom the year after seed is sown, but two or three years is the norm and it can be longer. Then you can check the identity of species, particularly those of sections that interbreed very readily, and name them only if you are sure they are right. Hybrids are unlikely to breed true but can give exciting results which spur you to try hybridizing yourself.

Hybridizing

Hybridizing is fascinating, possibly addictive, and taps a creative vein not always satisfied by other gardening activities. The most successful crosses are those between related parents, such as tall bearded × tall bearded and Japanese × Japanese, as they lead to further generations. Way-out crosses are more difficult and can give interesting, but often sterile, seedlings.

Choose the pod (female) and pollen (male) parents. On a dry day, remove their anthers and falls (p.14) as they begin to open

Dramatic colouring in 'space age' tall bearded 'Trillion' is emphasized by the long, upward-curving horns.

and before insects can get at them. The pollen parent's anthers should be closed but after a few hours in a dry place they will open to release the pollen grains; by then the stigmas on the pod parent should have bent forward, indicating that they are receptive. Holding an anther with tweezers, gently brush it across the stigma's upper surface (the side previously pressed against the style arm) and repeat with the other anthers and stigmas. The deposited pollen will be visible. Write the cross on a label (pod parent's name **x** pollen parent's name), tie it to the stem and record the details in your stud book.

Crosses may not 'take' in hot, dry weather, or on wet days when moisture bursts the pollen grains. Wait for better conditions and try again.

The ovary should start to swell quite soon, and about three months later the pod will begin to split at the top. Harvest the seeds and sow them as described above. When the seedlings flower, enjoy them, and if you would like to enter any in RHS or BIS trials, seek the advice of the judges.

PESTS AND DISEASES

PESTS

Slugs and snails are usually the worst pests and should be controlled by whatever method you prefer. Chewed leaves and flowers are unsightly and holes in rhizomes can admit diseases. Keep numbers down by removing possible hiding places: pull dead foliage gently away from the rhizomes and cut the leaves of deciduous beardless irises back to 15cm (6in) or less in autumn; the remains will come away easily in spring.

Aphids are unattractive and spread viruses. Insecticides based on bifenthrin. imidacloprid, derris or pyrethrum are available to amateur gardeners to keep aphids under control. As sprays kill beneficial insects too, try to spray when only aphids are active. Moth larvae and thrips, and iris sawfly, which can attack water-side irises, may pose problems although they are not usually widespread.

Vine weevil is reported as having killed Japanese irises in Devon, both in pots and the open ground. If these or other irises are attacked, treat container-grown plants with imidacloprid or use biological control with the vine weevil nematode. Only the latter treatment can be used on plants growing in the open ground.

Leaves and rhizomes can be eaten by rabbits, voles, mice or deer, and, on lighter soils, ants' nests under plants may result in poor growth. Discourage such pests by whatever means are practicable.

DISEASES

Diseases can be hard to control as plants are affected before any symptoms are visible. Bacterial soft rot is one of the commonest, especially among bearded irises if grown in poorly drained soil or a damp climate, or there is a long spell of wet weather. Rhizome damage caused by slugs allows the bacteria to enter, and the first sign is often yellowing of the leaf tips, then the whole fan falling over or coming away if it is grasped, showing a foul-smelling, yellowish mush at its base, spreading from the rhizome. Cut back to clean white tissue, scrape the soil away from all cut surfaces and dust them with green or yellow sulphur. Dispose of all infected material, by burning if possible – never put it on the compost heap – sterilize your knife and wash your hands thoroughly.

Warm, moist weather encourages several fungal diseases: leaf spot on the leaves of bearded irises, botrytis (grey mould) on some beardless irises and rust on both types. With leaf spot, small black blotches rapidly enlarge until the leaf withers away. Rust is usually less serious. Spray with myclobutanil or penconazole to control these problems. The same treatment should be given for botrytis, which reveals itself when the leaves of beardless irises go yellow, then brown, and collapse, and grey mould is visible at the base of the fans. Siberian cultivars seem most prone to suffer, particularly mass plantings on heavy ground, but it is rare if irises are mixed with other perennials. Preventive sprays given before any signs appear may help with control if either disease has occurred before.

Premature yellowing of leaves of Reticulatas or other bulbous irises is a sign of ink disease for which there is, at present, no cure. Dig up the bulbs, and if they have black spots or streaks, burn or dispose of them and the leaves. Do not plant new bulbs in the same places unless the soil has been sterilized.

Iris mosaic and other viruses can be spread by aphids or through the use of infected tools. Mild attacks have little or no effect but if leaves and flowers are badly marked or deformed, dig up the plants and dispose of them – there is no cure. Take care to buy uninfected plants.

Further Information

Books

Those marked ★ are out of print, but may be available through second-hand dealers.

The Gardener's Guide to Growing Irises, Geoff Stebbings (David & Charles, Timber Press, 2001)

The Gardener's Iris Book, William Shear (The Taunton Press, 1998)

The Genus Iris, W.R. Dykes 1913 (Facsimile edition, Dover Books 1975)

Growing Irises, G.E. Cassidy & S. Linnegar (Christopher Helm 1988)★

A Guide to Species: Irises, Ed. The Species Group of the British Iris Society (Cambridge University Press 1997)

The Iris, Brian Mathew, 2nd edition (Batsford 1989)★

Iris of China, James Waddick & Zhao Yu-tang (Timber Press, 1992)

Iris, Flower of the Rainbow, Graeme Grosvenor (Kangaroo Press Pty Ltd., 1987)

Iris, Fritz Kohlein (Ulmer, 1981; Christopher Helm, 1988; translated by Timber Press 1987)★

Iris, the Classic Bearded Varieties, Claire Austin (Quadrille Publishing Ltd., 2001)

Irises, A Practical Gardening Guide, Karen Glasgow (Godwit Publishing Ltd., NZ, 1996; Batsford, UK, 1997)

L'Iris, Une Fleur Royale, Richard Cayeux (Mauryflor, 1996)

The Japanese Iris, Currier McEwen (University Press of New England, 1990)

The Louisiana Iris, Ed. The Society for Louisiana Irises, 2nd Edition (Timber Press, 2000)

The Siberian Iris, Currier McEwen (Timber Press, 1992)

Societies

The British Iris Society (BIS)

Hon. Secretary, 40 Willow Park, Otford, Sevenoaks, Kent, TN14 5NF. Tel: 01959 523017
Email: hilarytowers@aol.com
Website:
www.britishirissociety.org.uk
The BIS publishes *The Iris Year Book* annually, as well as booklets on cultivation and other subjects, newsletters and a seed list. Regional and specialist groups. Shows and meetings. Extensive library available to members.

The American Iris Society (AIS)

Sara R. Marley, Secretary, 843 Co. Rd. 3, Hannibal, NY 13074, USA. Website: www.irises.org
The AIS publishes The Bulletin (four times a year), there are also regional societies and specialist sections.

Iris Society of Australia

c/o Mr J. Roberts, PO Box 457, Emerald, Victoria 3782, Australia

New Zealand Iris Society

Hon. Secretary, 25 Lucknow Road, Havelock North, New Zealand

Addresses of iris societies in other countries may be obtained from the BIS Hon. Membership Secretary, 15 Parkwood Drive, Rawtenstall, Lancashire.

Places to Visit

RHS Garden Wisley, Woking, Surrey GU23 6QB Tel. 01483 224234; fax: 01483 211750
Website: www.rhs.org.uk/gardens

Royal Botanic Gardens Kew, Richmond, Surrey TW9 3AB
Tel: 020 8332 5000
Website: www.rbgkew.org.uk

Royal Botanic Gardens Kew, Wakehurst Place, Ardingly, West Sussex, RH17 6TN
Tel: 01444 894100
Website: www.rbgkew.org.uk

BIS Garden at The Gardens of the Rose, Royal National Rose Society, Chiswell Green, St. Albans, Hertfordshire, AL2 3NR
Opening dates variable.
Tel: 01727 850461

Lingen Nursery and Garden, Lingen, Bucknell, Shropshire, SY7 0DY. Tel: 01544 267720
Website: www.lingennursery.co.uk
National Collection of *Iris sibirica* cultivars (NCCPG).

Rowden Gardens, Brentor, Tavistock, Devon PL19 0NG
Tel: 01822 810275
National Collection of Water Irises (NCCPG).

Marwood Hill Gardens,
Marwood, Barnstaple, Devon,
EX31 4EB Tel: 01271 42528
National Collection of *Iris ensata*
(NCCPG).

R.D. Nutt, Great Barfield,
Bradenham, High Wycombe,
Buckinghamshire, HP14 4HP
Tel: 01494 563741
National Collection of *Iris
unguicularis* (NCCPG).

SUPPLIERS
UNITED KINGDOM

Aulden Farm, Aulden,
Leominster, Herefordshire, HR6
0JT. Tel: 01568 720129
Website: www.auldenfarm.co.uk.
Iris ensata. No mail order.

Claire Austin Hardy Plants,
The Stone House, Cramp Pool,
Shifnal, Shropshire, TF11 8PE
Tel: 01952 463700
Website: www.claireaustin-
hardyplants.co.uk. Wide range.

Avon Bulbs, Burnt House
Farm, Mid Lambrook, South
Petherton, Somerset, TA13 5HE
Tel: 01460 242177
Website: www.avonbulbs.co.uk.
Bulbs, PCIs, Siberians.

Beeches Nursery, Village
Centre, Ashdon, Saffron Waldon,
Essex, CB10 2HB

Tel: 01799 584362. Wide range.

Broadleigh Gardens, Bishop's
Hull, Taunton, Somerset, TA4
1AE. Tel: 01823 286231
Website:
www.broadleighbulbs.co.uk.
Bulbs, Pacific Coast irises, SDBs,
species.

Cambridge Bulbs, 40
Whittlesford Road, Newton,
Cambridge, CB2 5PH
Tel: 01223 871760. Arils,
Arilbreds, bulbs, species.

Cotswold Garden Plants, Sands
Lane, Badsey, Evesham,
Worcestershire, WR11 5EZ
Tel: 01386 422829
Website: www.cgf.net. Bearded
and beardless.

Croftway Nursery, Yapton
Road, Barnham, Bognor Regis,
West Sussex, PO22 0BQ
Tel: 01243 552121
Website: www.croftway.co.uk.
Beardeds, Siberians.

Barry Emmerson, 24 Seaward
Avenue, Leiston, Suffolk, IP16
4BB, Tel: 01728 832650. Tall
bearded.

Famecheck Special Plants,
Hilltrees, Wandlebury Hill,
Cambridge, CB2 4AD.
Tel: 01223 243734. Beardeds.

The Iris Garden, 47 Station Road, Barnet, Hertfordshire, EN5 1PR. Tel: 0208 441 1300 Website: www.theirisgarden.co.uk. Tall and other bearded, spurias.

Kelways, Barrymore Farm, Langport, Somerset, TA10 9EZ Tel: 01458 250521 Website: www.kelways.co.uk. Wide range.

Lingen Nursery and Garden, Lingen, Bucknell, Shropshire, SY7 0DY, Tel: 01544 267720 Website: www.lingennursery.co.uk Siberians, bulbs, shorter beardeds.

Potterton & Martin, The Cottage Nursery, Moortown Road, Nettleton, Caistor, Lincolnshire, LN7 6HX Tel: 01472 851714 Website: www.users.globalnet.co.uk/~pottin. Arils, bulbs, species.

Rowden Gardens, Brentor, Tavistock, Devon, PL19 0NG Tel: 01822 810275. *Iris ensata*, water irises.

Seagate Irises, Long Sutton By-pass, Long Sutton, Lincolnshire, PE12 9RX. Tel: 01406 365138 Website: www.irises.co.uk. Beardeds.

Westonbirt Plants, 9 Westonbirt Close, Worcester, WR5 3RX Tel: 01905 350429. Bulbs, PCIs, species.

Zephyrwude Irises, 48 Blacker Lane, Crigglestone, Wakefield, West Yorkshire, WF4 3EW Tel: 01924 252101. Beardeds.

EUROPE
Cayeux S.A., Boite Postale 35, 45501 GIEN Cedex, France. Tel: 0800 096 4811 Website: www.cayeux.fr. Beardeds.

Dr T. Tamberg, Zimmerstr. 3, 12207 Berlin, Germany Tel: (0049)(0)30 712 4235 Website: http://home.t-online.de/home/Dr.T.u.C.Tamberg/. Siberians, beardless hybrids.

USA
Cooley's Iris Gardens, P.O. Box 126, Silverton, Oregon 97381-0126. Beardeds.

Schreiner's Iris Gardens, 3629 Quinaby Road, Salem, Oregon 97303. Wide range.

Many other iris nurseries advertise in the AIS Bulletin, which can be borrowed from the BIS Library by members.

INDEX

Page numbers in **bold** refer to illustrations

Acknowledgements:

Illustrations: Patrick Mulrey
Copy-editor: Jo Weeks
RHS editor: Simon Maughan
Proofreader: Rae Spencer-Jones
Index: Sue Bosanko

The publisher would like to thank the following people for their
kind permission to reproduce their photographs:

Cover image: The Garden Picture Library (John Glover)

B.C. Baughen: page 42

Jennifer Hewitt: pages 6, 7, 10 (bottom), 11, 22, 27, 37, 41, 45, 48, 50, 51, 52, 53, 55,
56, 57, 60, 63, 65, 73, 77, 89

Sidney Linnegar: pages 2, 4, 9 (top and bottom), 10 (top), 17, 19, 21, 24, 28, 31, 32,
34, 36, 39, 54, 58, 59, 61, 69, 71, 74, 79, 80, 83

Hiroshi Shimizu: page 67

F. J. Webbing: pages 35, 36, 44, 64, 68

The Iris Garden: page 85